BACKP... LIFE LIST

The Magazine Of Wilderness Travel

THE 50 ULTIMATE HIKING ADVENTURES

BY THE EDITORS OF
BACKPACKER MAGAZINE

RODALE

© 2003 by Rodale Inc.

All rights reserved. No part of this publication may be reproduced or transmitted in any form or by any means, electronic or mechanical, including photocopying, recording, or any other information storage and retrieval system, without the written permission of the publisher.

Backpacker is a registered trademark of Rodale Inc.

Printed in the United States of America
Rodale Inc. makes every effort to use acid-free ∞ , recycled paper ♻ .

Book design by Drew Frantzen

Library of Congress Cataloging-in-Publication Data

Backpacker life list : the 50 ultimate hiking adventures / by
the editors of Backpacker magazine.
p.   cm.
ISBN 1–57954–804–0 paperback
1. Hiking—Guidebooks.   I. Backpacker.
GV199.5.B33   2003
796.51—dc22   2003015005

Distributed to the book trade by St. Martin's Press

2   4   6   8   10   9   7   5   3   1   paperback

FOR MORE OF OUR PRODUCTS
WWW.RODALESTORE.COM
(800) 848-4735

RODALE
WE INSPIRE AND ENABLE PEOPLE TO IMPROVE
THEIR LIVES AND THE WORLD AROUND THEM

Visit us on the Web at www.rodalestore.com or www.backpacker.com,

or call us toll-free at (800) 848-4735.

Contents

Introduction

Warning: This book may be disruptive to your daily routine.

In extensive field trials, the stories and trip planners contained herein have been shown to produce incurable bouts of restlessness and extreme wanderlust. Other symptoms include uncontrollable daydreaming, long lunches at the local outdoors store, and furtive searching for the lowest fares to faraway airports.

But what's more important: your everyday responsibilities or a life well-lived? We think it's the latter, which is why the editors of BACKPACKER magazine bring you this collection of the natural world's greatest hits. In the pages that follow, you'll find 50 extraordinary adventures that belong on every hiker's life list. Yellowstone. Glacier. Yosemite. The Inca Trail. Here are the great treks and wild parks—the famous (and a few not-so-famous) places where you can experience abundant scenery, solitude, and wildlife.

Every one of these adventures will alter your spiritual DNA. We know, because we've been out there, and we haven't been the same since. So tell your boss, your teachers, or your parents to back off next time they catch you daydreaming. Starting now, you have places to go. And not many people to see.

—Jonathan Dorn
Executive Editor
BACKPACKER magazine

ADIRONDACK MOUNTAINS, NEW YORK

Breathe easy (or hard) in the Empire State's highland paradise

To spend a clear fall evening in the Adirondack Mountains is to know serenity. You move among brilliant stands of birch and maple, as curtains of yellow, red, and orange leaves dance and shimmer in the breeze. In the distance, a deer and her fawn weave between the trees. Every breath takes in pine-scented, crystalline air. And there's not a bug or cloud in the sky.

The company you keep along the marble- and quartz-studded trails here is up to you. Crowds rush for the High Peaks region to challenge 5,344-foot Mount Marcy, the highest point in New York. But if a throng of human faces isn't your idea of wilderness scenery, leave the area's bigger summits to the crowds. Opt instead for a multiday loop that starts at Johns Brook Lodge and ambles along the Phelps Trail, passing martens, fishers, and photogenic Johns Brook. If you're lucky, you'll catch a glimpse of those black bears around Marcy Dam; regardless of luck, you'll climb the Phelps to a clearing where 5,114-foot Mount Algonquin towers above the panorama. Then hit the Range Trail toward Haystack Mountain. Here, the scenery comes at a price: Get ready for a rugged, butt-busting circuit of six (eight if you're ambitious) 4,000-foot peaks. But the returns are worth it. Expect sharp ledges, plenty of exposure, and classic Adirondack views of the Catskill Mountains, Vermont, and Canada.

FIELD JOURNAL

Expedition Planner

★PERMITS: Though a permit isn't necessary for hiking or backcountry camping, you do need a pass to stay in one of the 20 Department of Environmental Conservation–operated campgrounds. Reserve a site by calling (800) 456-2500.

★ACCESS: The Phelps Trail is located 280 miles north of Manhattan. Take exit 30 off I-87, and follow US 9/NY 73 north toward Keene Valley, New York. In Keene Valley, turn left onto Adirondack Street. After 0.6 mile, the road veers right and continues over a wooden bridge and up a hill. Follow signs for The Garden. Parking is $5 a day. The trail to the Johns Brook Lodge (518-523-3441) is well marked; the Phelps Trail begins near the lodge.

★SEASON: The period from Memorial Day to Labor Day is the park's high season. Locals prefer the spring or fall for the beauty and serenity of the trails.

*GEAR: Temperatures drop during frequent summer storms. Always carry raingear, a wool sweater, a hat, and gloves in your pack, even on a warm day. Expect snow anytime from late October through May.

*GUIDE SERVICES: Trails are well marked, so a guide is unnecessary.

*GUIDEBOOKS AND MAPS: The Adirondack Mountain Club's Guide to Adirondack Trails (with map), (Adirondack Mountain Club, 800-395-8080, $16.95).

*CONTACT: The New York State Department of Environmental Conservation, Region 5 (518-897-1200); High Peaks Information Center (518-523-3441), operated by the Adirondack Mountain Club.

ALGONQUIN PROVINCIAL PARK, ONTARIO

The water's edge is alive in Canada's premier paddling park

Thirty minutes and 500 strokes of the paddle, and already your goal is complete: Your canoe is not a field's distance from the biggest, fullest set of antlers you've ever seen. This is Algonquin Provincial Park, nestled in the heart of Ontario, where the north country's evergreen forests meet the south's maples and birches in a frenzy of nature. The antlers belong to a brown moose the size of a Durango, lunching on prickly rose by the edge of a cedar bog.

Algonquin is a place where all of the wildlife that's supposed to be there is still there. Where doses of white-tailed deer, beavers, gray jays, and turtles living in sylvan solitude are a daily possibility. Where you can camp be-

side a lake, look north, and know that the forest extends uninterrupted for hundreds of miles. In this place, you'll find remoteness and wilderness without the heart-pounding elevation changes that come with most of the truly wild locales in the United States.

And chances are you'll find these things while traveling in a canoe. The park has only 14 day-hikes and three backcountry trails (most are accessible from ON 60), but it has miles and miles of flat water. Pick a pond, lake, or marsh—and launch. Before long, the show will begin. A ripple next to your boat might turn out to be an otter. The wind may carry the whistle of a thrush. And, come nightfall, your heart will skip five beats when the wolves sing to you across the still waters in the moonlight.

FIELD JOURNAL

with temperatures sometimes dipping below freezing.

*GEAR: Rent just about everything you'll need for a backcountry canoe trip—from the boat and life jackets to the sleeping bags, stove, and guide—from Algonquin Outfitters (705-635-2243), outside the west gate of the park in Whitney, with a seasonal location (613-637-2075) inside the east gate on Lake Opeongo. Opeongo Outfitters (613-637-5470), outside the east gate in Dwight, and the Portage Store (705-633-5622), inside the west gate, also offer rentals and guides.

*GUIDE SERVICES: Algonquin Outfitters is the most popular service, but all three mentioned above host trips.

*GUIDEBOOKS AND MAPS: *Algonquin Canoe Routes* (Friends of Algonquin, 613-637-2828, $4.95 [Canadian]); *Algonquin Backpacking Trails Map* (Friends of Algonquin, 613-637-2828, $1.95 [Canadian]).

*CONTACT: Algonquin Provincial Park (705-633-5572).

ALPINE LAKES WILDERNESS, WASHINGTON

Boldly go where very few are allowed to go

Ever visit the moon? Hike to the upper reaches of the Enchantment Basin, and you'll come close. The path that takes you here traverses the Alpine Lakes Wilderness like a staircase into space. You climb into earthy woodland groves, past lakes as clear as the stratosphere, and onto the Lost World Plateau, where you stand among rock gardens of jagged peaks, basking in your own sea of tranquility.

The tricky part is getting here. The trail is a natural obstacle course of very steep terrain, with elevation gains of 4,000 to 6,000 feet in just a few miles. Add the difficulty of getting a permit—the Wilderness offers only 20 each day—and you'll understand why many hikers have abandoned their Enchantment dreams in favor of more accessible scrambles.

Be patient and resolved, however, and you'll have the chance to revel in a quiet, fragile landscape unlike anywhere else on the planet. From the Snow Lake trailhead, you'll hike past ancient valleys of whitebark pine and subalpine larch and into the rugged alpine tundra of the Washington Cascades. The first of many lakes, snow lingering on its banks, stirs in the slow mountain wind. Mountain goats prowl the rocky basin as you move up the stair-stepped Lower Enchantments, from the fabled Gnome Tarn, with its classic views of craggy Prusik Peak, to the King Arthur's Legends Lakes. Past each lake, another lake. Behind each peak, another peak. Finally, 8,000 feet up, you reach the cusp of the Lost World. One small step, and you have arrived.

FIELD JOURNAL

Expedition Planner

★PERMITS: Permits cost $3 per person per day. They are available through the Leavenworth Ranger Station (see "Contact," below). A quota is in effect from June 15 to October 15. Make your reservations by mail in late February or in person beginning March 1. The ranger station saves five individual permits for walk-ins and distributes them through a lottery at 7:45 A.M. daily. Day use is handled through self-issued permits at trailheads. A Northwest Forest Pass ($5 a day or $30 a year) is required to park at any trailhead.

★ACCESS: The route into the Enchantments begins 130 miles east of Seattle. For the Snow Creek trailhead, take US 2 in Leavenworth, Washington, to Icicle Creek Road. Follow this for 4 miles to the parking lot on your left. The Colchuck Lake trailhead is 8 miles farther down the road.

★SEASON: Ideal hiking is from August through mid-September, to avoid the snow and snowmelt.

★GEAR: No special gear is necessary.

★GUIDE SERVICES: None.

★GUIDEBOOKS AND MAPS: *100 Hikes in Washington's Alpine Lakes*, by Ira Spring, Vicky Spring, and Harvey Manning (The Mountaineers Books, 800-553-4453, $16.95); *The Enchantments, #209S* (Green Trails, 206-546-6277, $3.60).

★CONTACT: Alpine Lakes Wilderness Hotline (800-627-0062); Leavenworth Ranger Station (600 Sherbourne, Leavenworth, WA 98826; 509-548-6977).

ANNAPURNA CIRCUIT, NEPAL

This trek across Nepal is your path to the rooftop of the world

You're on a trail where you can see terraced farmland climbing impossibly steep mountainsides. You step aside to allow a yak train to pass and tip your hat to porters bent under monstrous loads. In the distance, you hear the thunder of avalanches as you eat lunch at a lonely teahouse at 13,000 feet. Inside a stone temple built into the foot of an imposing cliff, a stooped, aged monk blesses your journey. You tentatively cross narrow footbridges that sway above raging rivers, and pass through villages of stone huts where children laugh and play, and people live as they have for centuries. At a mountain pass,

Buddhist prayer flags whip in the wind.

This is not a dream. This is the Annapurna Circuit, a 17- to 25-day trek around Nepal's lofty Annapurna range. If the Himalaya—hands down the biggest, most majestic mountains in the world—has the best hiking anywhere, then this is the single hike that tops them all. The path winds through stepped rice paddies and over monstrous gorges, taking you 17,000 feet up and permitting a kiss-close view of the Dhaulagiri and Annapurna summits (each more than 26,000 feet high). And while you may hike to get away from the crowds back at home, visitors to the Himalaya often love its inhabitants and its scenery equally. Revel in this opportunity for a natural and cultural adventure—they don't come together often enough.

FIELD JOURNAL

Expedition Planner

★**PERMITS:** You will need a visa to enter Nepal; obtain one at the airport or at one of the embassies in the United States. Trekking permits are required: pick one up in Kathmandu or Pokhara.

★**ACCESS:** There is an airport at Pokhara, but most trekkers fly to Kathmandu, take a bus, and start their journey in Besisahar. From here, the trek lasts about 16 days. You'll end in Pokhara and then fly back to Kathmandu.

★**SEASON:** From October through November, the skies are clear, the valleys are warm and flower filled, and the higher elevations may get snow. Rhododendron forests bloom in spring. Don't attempt to cross 17,700-foot Thorung La Pass in bad weather.

★**GEAR:** Pack a sleeping pad and three-season bag, but leave the tent and cooking gear home. There are plenty of teahouses or "hotels" that offer meals and a bed with a thin mattress. Carry water treatment equipment.

★**GUIDE SERVICES:** You can do this trek unguided or find a licensed trekking service in Kathmandu's Thamel District. A good guide service based in the United States is Mountain Travel Sobek (888-687-6235).

★**GUIDEBOOKS AND MAPS:** *Trekking in Nepal: A Traveler's Guide* (includes maps), by Stephen Bezruchka (The Mountaineers Books, 800-553-4453, $16.95).

★**CONTACT:** Royal Nepalese Embassy in Washington, DC (202-667-4550).

ANSEL ADAMS WILDERNESS, CALIFORNIA

Discover the light that inspired a legend

In 1916, Ansel Adams saw the light. At 14 years old, on a family trip to a wilderness region in California, he was taken at once by the unbounded space, the smell of the pines, the deep shadows, the cliffs rising to "undreamed of heights," and all that light—one moment cutting and dark, then suddenly soft and bright, nearly pastel.

It was all "so intense as to be almost painful," he would later say. "I knew my destiny when I first experienced Yosemite."

Next door, in his namesake wilderness, you may experience the same revelation Adams did on another trip, after which he wrote, "I saw more clearly than I have ever seen before or since the minute detail of the grasses, the clusters of sand shifting in the wind, the small flotsam of the forest, the motion of the high clouds

streaming above the peaks. There are no words to convey the moods of those moments."

To visit the 230,258-acre Ansel Adams Wilderness is to confront the truth and beauty captured in his photography. Here you'll find the meadows with blossoms dancing in the breeze, the red fir like ladders into the sky, the high mountain passes layered in late afternoon sun, the diamonds of light splashing in rushing streams.

Several paths will take you into the best parts of Ansel Adams Wilderness, but try the sparsely traveled, 23.7-mile, one-way Koip Peak Pass Traverse. You'll follow Adams's magic light across four mountain passes, through lingering snowfields, around five alpine lakes, and into fragrant fields. Be prepared to exercise your legs. And your shutter finger.

FIELD JOURNAL

Expedition Planner

★PERMITS: Permits are required for overnight camping; pick up a self-issued one at the trailhead. From May 1 to November 1, trails have entry quotas for overnight hikers. Reserve a spot by phone (see "Contact," opposite page), or apply for a next-day permit at any forest ranger station at 11 A.M. the day before you plan to enter the park. The wilderness office saves 40 percent of the permits for walk-ins. The Ansel Adams Wilderness straddles the Sierra and Inyo National Forests; permits are based on the starting trailhead.

★ACCESS: To get to the Koip Peak Pass Traverse from US 395, take CA 158 and drive until you get to Silver Lake. The trail begins at the horse corrals to your left.

★SEASON: For the best hiking, head out between late June and late September.

★GEAR: Bear-resistant canisters are mandatory for overnight trips from May 25 through October 31. Rent one at the visitor center. Sudden mountain storms are common throughout the year. Carry extra food and dry clothing.

★**GUIDE SERVICES:** None.

★**GUIDEBOOKS AND MAPS:** *Yosemite Park and Vicinity* (Wilderness Press, 800-443-7227, $6.95); *100 Hikes in California's Central Sierra and Coast Range*, by Vicky Spring (The Mountaineers Books, 800-553-4453, $12.95).

★**CONTACT:** For east side entry (June Lake Loop to Tioga Pass, Inyo National Forest, Mono Lake Ranger District), call (760) 647-3044. For east side entry (Red Meadow to Agnew Meadow, Inyo National Forest, Mammoth Ranger District, Highway 203), call (760) 924-5500. For west side entry north of the San Joaquin River (Sierra National Forest, Bass Lake Ranger District), call (559) 877-2218. For west side entry south of the San Joaquin River (Sierra National Forest, High Sierra Ranger District), call (559) 855-5355.

APPALACHIAN TRAIL

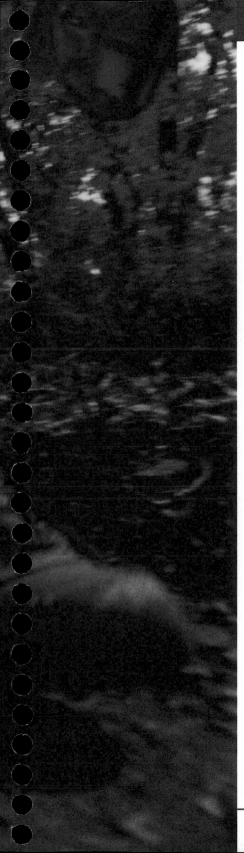

America's classic is a trip into the past

Are you ready to walk 2,172 miles?

It's okay to say no. While anyone who hikes the path from Springer Mountain in Georgia to Mount Katahdin in Maine deserves praise (not to mention a good foot massage), of the more than 4 million people who enjoy the Appalachian Trail each year, only about 500 complete it. The others settle for a brief encounter with some of the oldest, richest stone ever to push through the North American soil.

No matter where you hit the AT, you'll find history waiting. The peaks of the Appalachian chain were ancient and round before the jagged Cascades rose. In the beds of mountain streams and lakes sit the fossilized remains of some of the planet's oldest organisms. Among the mixed forests, rock ridges, bald summits and—depending on the season—spring flowers or crisp foliage, you'll see the remnants of long-forgotten cemeteries and stumble over rubble from Revolutionary War–era iron mines. You may pass through a Pennsylvania clearing where, in the 1600s, settlers hunted wild turkey; or into a Virginia gully where Union and Confederate troops battled; or over the Georgia mountain where, legend has it, Native Americans once fought a war so bloody it turned nearby rivers red. And when you hear the moan of a coal train in the distant Tennessee hills, the billows from a steam engine will drift through your mind's eye, if not the sky.

FIELD JOURNAL

_____
_____
_____
_____
_____
_____
_____
_____
_____
_____
_____
_____
_____
_____
_____
_____
_____
_____
_____
_____
_____
_____

Expedition Planner

*PERMITS: There are no permits for hiking the AT, but, unless you're a thru-hiker, you will need one to stay overnight in shelters or designated campsites in Great Smoky Mountains National Park in Tennessee and North Carolina, Shenandoah National Park in Virginia, White Mountain National Forest in New Hampshire, and Baxter State Park in Maine. Check with the parks for fee information.

*ACCESS: There are more than 500 access points stretched across 14 states, from Maine to Georgia.

*SEASON: For the best times to hike in specific states, consult the AT's Web site, www.appalachiantrail.org. Thru-hikers should begin in Georgia and head north, as the weather is more favorable. You can start in Georgia in March; in Maine, you'd have to wait until June. However, the thru-hike's popularity has skyrocketed in recent years. If you're going to launch a thru-hike from Georgia

APPALACHIAN TRAIL

in March or the first half of April, be aware that there will be lots and lots of people on the trail. Shelters might be full; paths crowded.

★GEAR: Bring a good, comfortable backpack and a lightweight tent. Pack as light as possible, as the journey is really a series of shorter trips strung together. You don't need to pack for 2,000-plus miles, just for your first 30. Every 3 to 5 days, you'll come to a town or place where you can replenish your supplies.

★GUIDES: None.

★GUIDEBOOKS AND MAPS: The Appalachian Trail Conference set of guidebooks and topographical maps will cover all of your needs (888-287-8673).

★CONTACT: Appalachian Trail Conference (304-535-6331).

ARCTIC NATIONAL WILDLIFE REFUGE, ALASKA

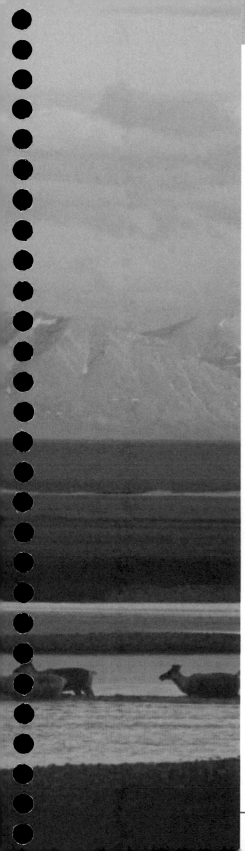

Track the wild life in a land where the sun never sets

It's easy to feel insignificant when you travel deep into a refuge that could hold 10 Yellowstones. When rows of nameless peaks crowd the horizon, and you find yourself smack in the middle of the calving grounds of a Porcupine caribou herd 120,000 members strong. When the land before you holds bears that could flip an SUV with a few smacks of the paw. When the mid-June sun sets for only a sliver of the day, shining softly like a night-light, and the mosquitoes get so thick you kill two dozen with a single slap.

But if moments of grace are what you seek, you're as likely to find them in the Arctic National Wildlife Refuge as you are anywhere on the planet.

There are no roads or trails here, but in this open land a path isn't necessary. Strike out cross-country, following a compass bearing over the tundra. You also might want to follow a caribou trail through the gravelly river valleys, then up the mountains on the north slope of the Brooks Range. In the quiet of a midnight sun, you might see wisps of fog off the Arctic Ocean working their way across the coastal plain. The vapor moves into the shadows of the cliffs and disappears, then wafts into a shaft of sunlight between two spires of rock. It glows with a swirl of rainbow colors, only to reach the next shadow and vanish so quickly it makes you gasp. And to think there's another vision of untamed wilderness just around the bend. And another, until you almost can't bear the pleasure of North America's last great frontier.

 # FIELD JOURNAL

_____

_____

_____

_____

_____

_____

_____

_____

_____

_____

_____

_____

_____

_____

_____

_____

_____

_____

_____

Expedition Planner

★**PERMITS:** None.

★**ACCESS:** Commercial airlines serve Arctic Village, Dead Horse, Fort Yukon, and Kaktovik, which are jumping-off points for most ANWR trips. Bush planes take you the rest of the way. Contact the refuge manager (See "Contact," opposite page) for a list of bush plane operators. Out of Arctic Village, try Yukon Air (907-479-3792 or 907-662-2445).

★**SEASON:** Winter comes early and stays late. You'll encounter ice in passes and streams well into June, and snow may fall year-round. There's relatively little precipitation, and most of it falls as summer rain. But be ready for cold, wet, windy conditions any time of year. Since the sun doesn't set between mid-May and early August, there's plenty of daylight to wait out bad weather.

★**GEAR:** It's legal to carry firearms in the refuge. Pepper spray may also be brought in; however, some bush pilots won't allow it in the plane or will require that you keep it in an airtight container while in flight.

★GUIDE SERVICES: For less experienced hikers, a list of guide services is available from the refuge manager (see "Contact," at right).

★GUIDEBOOKS AND MAPS: While guidebooks are hard to come by, there is a lot of passionate writing about ANWR. Try *Arctic Refuge: A Circle of Testimony*, by Hank Lentfer and Carolyn Servid (Milkweed Editions, 612-332-3192; $14), and *Midnight Wilderness: Journeys in Alaska's Arctic National Wildlife Refuge*, by Debbie S. Miller and Margaret Murie (Alaska Northwest Books, 907-278-8838, $14.95). Because the area is so huge, no single map provides the scale needed to navigate. Ask the refuge manager for more information.

★CONTACT: Refuge Manager (800-362-4546 or 907-456-0250).

ARIZONA TRAIL, ARIZONA

Cooler weather makes a heaven of hell

It's not the longest trail in the United States. It's certainly not the oldest. It probably won't amaze your friends (unless you brave it during the Arizona summer) or shock your parents or children. You won't even cross one state line, let alone a dozen, while traveling it.

But if mind-splitting beauty is enough for you, then by all means tackle the longest thru-hike in the Southwest. The Arizona Trail is every outdoorsman's connect-the-dots fantasy: For a mere pittance (time, some boot rubber, a run-in with the occasional rattlesnake), you can buy passage through a state's worth of seminal scrambles and canyons, tied together along a challenging but surmountable course.

If you're a believer in starting out good and only getting better, begin at the lip of Mexico and go north. You'll soon hit Huachuca, the first of six mountain ranges, with its crusty peaks and views into forever. In the Sonoran Desert, you'll find cacti growing tall and sturdy. In the Kachina Peaks Wilderness, arrow-straight conifers shoot from the soil, their green branches loosely overlapping in mesh that seems to catch and tame the Arizona sun. The largest ponderosa forest in the world lies just beyond.

With so much to see, you may forget where you're actually headed. That is, until you reach your finale: the Grand Canyon, laying nearly half the earth's entire 4.5-billion-year history on its side and quietly glowing red, gold, and brown. One look and you are transformed: your feet are in Arizona; your mind has entered a state of ecstasy.

FIELD JOURNAL

Expedition Planner

★**PERMITS:** None.

★**ACCESS:** The 790-mile trail, marked with signposts, is accessible from 42 major trailheads spaced 15 to 20 miles apart from Mexico to Utah.

★**SEASON:** Hike the northern part of the trail from May to October, the southern part from October to May.

★**GEAR:** Water, sunscreen, lip balm.

★**GUIDE SERVICES:** Contact the Arizona Trail Association (see "Contact," below) for a list of guides and stewards to help you plan your hike and to stash water along the route ahead of your journey.

★**GUIDEBOOKS AND MAPS:** *Crossing Arizona: A Solo Hike through the Sky Islands and Deserts of the Arizona Trail*, by Chris Townsend (Countryman Press, 800-245-4151, $17.95).

★**CONTACT:** Arizona Trail Association (602-252-4794).

BADLANDS NATIONAL PARK, SOUTH DAKOTA

What's not to like about America's most brutal backcountry?

Enticing. Vicious. Picturesque. Unforgiving. The South Dakota Badlands have been called it all. Deserved it all, too. In this desert, rainbow buttes and otherworldly spires rise above the land, resting like gladiators after battle. Sometimes, you can almost hear the white clouds passing overhead. Other times, their voice is unmistakable, booming down in black thunderclaps from the sky like a reprimand: *You don't belong here.*

But you do. Within the quarter-million acres of Badlands National Park, you'll find treasures not to be missed. Away from the terrain of windshield tourists are square-edged hills of layer upon layer of clay and sandstone, and weather-sculpted formations that call to mind fortresses and castles. Out here, the prairie dogs play and squeak at passersby who get too close. The tree trunks are decorated with tufts of coarse brown hair left by itchy buffalo. The air is filled with song—meadowlarks during the day, coyotes at night—and the scent of sweet sage.

The park's 64,250-acre Badlands Wilderness Area (known to locals as the Sage Creek Wilderness) is ideal for cross-country backpacking, but be warned: The Badlands don't play fair. Lug as much water as you can. Prepare for encounters with grumpy bison. Watch for snakes. And before you sit down to rest, check the ground below. These Badlands are not above slipping a cactus beneath you.

FIELD JOURNAL

BADLANDS NATIONAL PARK, SD

Expedition Planner

★**PERMITS:** The entrance fee is $10 per vehicle for 7 days, $20 annually; or use your National Parks Pass or Golden Pass (Age, Eagle, and Access).

★**ACCESS:** Badlands is 50 miles east of Rapid City, South Dakota, and 270 miles east of Sioux Falls. From exit 110 or 131 off I-90, take Badlands Loop Road, SD 240, which ends at the park. Or follow SD 44, which also ends at the park.

★**SEASON:** Though crowds are thickest from Memorial Day through Labor Day, the prime hiking seasons are early spring and early fall. Summer heat can exceed 100°F, while winter days commonly drop to -30°F—without factoring in windchill.

★**GEAR:** None of the Badlands' water is potable, so bring your own. Open fires are not allowed, so you'll need a backpacker's stove.

★**GUIDE SERVICES:** None.

★**GUIDEBOOKS AND MAPS:** *Exploring the Black Hills and Badlands*, by Hiram Rogers (Johnson Books, 303-443-9766, $17); *Hiking South Dakota's Black Hills Country: A Falcon Guide*, by Bert and Jane Gildart (Globe Pequot Press, 800-243-0495, $14.95); *Badlands National Park #239* (National Geographic Trails Illustrated Maps, 800-962-1643, $9.95).

★**CONTACT:** Badlands National Park (605-433-5361).

BANFF NATIONAL PARK, ALBERTA

Lose youself in Canada's answer to Yellowstone

How big is Banff? Big enough that it holds the very best and the very worst of the Canadian Rockies within its 2,564 square miles.

Skeptics like to focus on the worst. They'll tell you this long, skinny park has become a wilderness shopping mall. They'll decry the hotels, the bowling alley, and the restaurants that have sprung up like concrete mushrooms. They'll say that development has left even uglier by-products: malfunctioning wastewater treatment plants, construction debris, roads, and electric and natural-gas lines; not to mention high-maintenance hikers who crowd a handful of the park's most magnificent trails. And they'll be right.

But Banff bashers forget the other 97 percent of the park, where the forests and mountain scenery rival Alaska's most secluded reaches. If you can't find a gorgeous, peaceful spot away from the minigolf courses, you haven't been looking very hard.

Let's say you find yourself in Lake Louise, one of Banff's most commercial (yet still beautiful) areas. Make your escape via the 20-mile trail through Skoki Valley. You'll cut through wide, lush meadows as you weave between the peaks of the Slate Range. When you hit Deception Pass, surreal mountain scenery will play tricks on your eyes. In Merlin Meadows, you'll tramp through alpine wildflowers that cover the fields as thickly as moss. And at night you'll relax under the stars after taking a polar bear swim in Lake Merlin. As full-body experiences go, there isn't a day spa in all of Lake Louise that compares.

FIELD JOURNAL

Expedition Planner

★**PERMITS:** Backcountry hikers must purchase a wilderness permit for $6 (Canadian) per person per night or $42 (Canadian) per person per year. Some designated campsites can be reserved up to 3 months ahead for $10 (Canadian) by calling the park (see "Contact," opposite page); the rest are allocated on a first come, first served basis.

★**ACCESS:** Calgary, Alberta, which is 80 miles (1½ hours) west of Banff National Park, has the closest international airport, and from there you have three options for getting to the park: Rent a car, hop on a bus to the town of Banff, or catch a ride with Brewster Transportation (403-762-6767), which will drop you off in the town of Banff, at Lake Louise, or at trailheads along the highway.

★**SEASON:** Plan to visit from July through September. Park staff at the visitor centers in the town of Banff and at Lake Louise can tell you which trails are snow-free. Early fall is a good time to go because there are fewer

_____
_____
_____
_____
_____
_____
_____
_____
_____
_____
_____
_____
_____
_____
_____
_____
_____
_____
_____
_____
_____
_____

bugs and fewer people on the trails, not to mention spectacular visual treats like the larches in all their autumnal glory.

⋆**GEAR:** Bring a backpacker's stove and a water treatment system. Bear spray is recommended.

⋆**GUIDE SERVICES:** Contact the park (see "Contact," at right) for a list of licensed guides.

⋆**GUIDEBOOKS AND MAPS:** *Backcountry Visitor's Guide* brochure; *The Canadian Rockies Trail Guide*, by Brian Patton and Bart Robinson (Summerthought Publishing, 403-762-3919, $14.95); *Classic Hikes in the Canadian Rockies*, by Graeme Pole (Altitude Publishing, 403-678-6888, $24.95); *Banff Up-Close* (Gem Trek Publishing, 403-932-4208, $9.95 [Canadian]). Topographic maps and trip-planning information are available from the Friends of Banff National Park by calling (403) 762-8918.

⋆**CONTACT:** Banff National Park Information Center (403-762-1550).

BAXTER STATE PARK, MAINE

Tackle the mountain at the top of the Appalachian Trail

In the predawn darkness, your headlamp illuminates the Abol Trail for a muscle-loosening mile through dense woods. You pass by a cow moose lapping gingerly at a brook. Soon gravel crunches underfoot—the beginning of Abol Slide.

Then you're beneath monolithic Mount Katahdin, and the climb begins in earnest. Lift those knees, breathe deeply, and watch for falling rocks. And when you get to the Tableland as the sun's first rays rise above the mountain, some 5,100 feet up, you take a breath and look out on a valley so big you mistake it for all of Maine.

As famous mountains go, Katahdin is the runt of the litter. In fact, some 43,349 people mounted its flanks in 2001. But that doesn't stop it from being one of the more inspiring—and, some would say, adventuresome—climbs east of the Mississippi. Daring hikers will take the Roaring Brook Trail up and onto the sharp ridge that connects two of Katahdin's highest summits, a natural bridge called Knife Edge. This bladelike pass, which looms 5,250 feet above the earth, a mere 6 feet wide at its narrowest point, is prized by mountain aficionados as a test of nerves. It may strike you in midcrossing that all this danger is just minutes away from the relative safety of the Appalachian Trail. But for the sake of anyone watching you, keep moving; there'll be time for ruminating when the Knife is behind you.

FIELD JOURNAL

_____
_____
_____
_____
_____
_____
_____
_____
_____
_____
_____
_____
_____
_____
_____
_____
_____
_____
_____
_____
_____
_____
_____
_____

Expedition Planner

*PERMITS: To reach the Abol Trail, you'll need to stay in the Abol Campground, on the west side of the park. The campground has a quota, requires reservations, and costs $8 per person per night. It has both lean-tos and tenting. Two brooks run through the campground, which hikers use for drinking water. Also, while foot entry into Baxter State Park is free, all nonresident vehicles must have a day pass or season pass to enter the park. The parking fee is $10 per vehicle per day, $32 for a season pass. If you're camping in the park, the fee covers your entire trip, since you entered the park only once. If you're camping outside the park and coming in each day, however, you'll pay $10 each time you enter. Expect moderate price increases in the future.

*ACCESS: For the Roaring Brook trailhead, take exit 56 off I-95 and follow ME 157 west for 12 miles into Millinocket. Turn onto Millinocket Lake Road and follow it for 17 miles to the Togue Pond Gate House, where you'll check in. For the

_____
_____
_____
_____
_____
_____
_____
_____
_____
_____
_____
_____
_____
_____
_____
_____
_____
_____
_____
_____
_____

Abol Trail, follow the left fork onto a dirt road for 6 miles; the Abol Campground is on your right.

*SEASON: For a one-day hike of Mount Katahdin, the season is mid-May to mid-October, though if you'd like to cross Knife Edge, come in July or August, when the weather's more suitable. You can also camp between December 1 and April 1 for a multiday hike up Katahdin.

*GEAR: Some campgrounds do not permit open fires. Call the park headquarters (see "Contact," below) to see if you should bring a gas or propane stove. You don't need special gear to cross Knife Edge; the wind can be unnerving, but you can bare-hand across.

*GUIDE SERVICES: None.

*GUIDEBOOKS AND MAPS: Call the park (see "Contact," below) for a copy of *Katahdin: A Guide to Baxter State Park and Katahdin*, by Stephen Clark (Clark Press, 207-723-5140, $21)

*CONTACT: Baxter State Park Headquarters (207-723-5140).

BEARTOOTH MOUNTAINS, MONTANA

If you'd die for great peaks, welcome to Nirvana

It's dawn, and the clopping drumbeat of hooves circles your tent as two mountain goats scamper across the rock-strewn tundra. Looking out, you watch them play follow-the-leader alongside a truck-size boulder as soft morning light spreads across the jagged peaks, snow-fields, and lakes of Montana's highest balcony, the Beartooth Mountains.

Dozens of Beartooth trails beckon hikers, but the views you'll encounter during a trip to Aero Lakes are hard to resist. Here, on a vast alpine table-land 10,000 feet up, the scenery stretches south into Yellowstone Park. Turn north, and Mount Villard and the dark, sawtooth crests of the Vil-

lard Spires rise above a mountain tarn. A scramble to the top of Villard's neighbor, Glacier Peak, tops a long list of attractive daytrips. Expect a panorama of ice-lined summits, including 12,799-foot Granite Peak, Montana's tallest.

On the way, you'll wander along the shores of a forest lake where tall, snowy precipices rise above the treetops. Flower-strewn meadows along Zimmer Creek's glacier-carved cirque lead to the route's only serious climb, nicknamed Cardiac Gulch. A striking transition occurs when you hit the top: As the last grove of trees gives way to a broad, open plateau, you'll revel at the million-acre collage before you.

FIELD JOURNAL

_____
_____
_____
_____
_____
_____
_____
_____
_____
_____
_____
_____
_____
_____
_____
_____
_____
_____
_____
_____
_____
_____

Expedition Planner

*PERMITS: None.

*ACCESS: The Fisher Creek trailhead is 2 miles north of Cooke City. Cooke City is in far south-central Montana, on Beartooth Highway, at the northeast corner of Yellowstone National Park. This is 150 miles southwest of Billings. From Cooke City, take US 212 east. Then follow Fisher Creek Road, a country gravel road, for 2 miles to the roughly marked trailhead.

*SEASON: Prime hiking season is from early July through September. Snow-covered slopes can be hazardous in early summer, and mosquitoes can be a concern until the first frost hits, typically in mid-August.

*GEAR: Sturdy hiking boots and trekking poles come in handy for rough spots. You may want to bring wading shoes for several minor fords. Wind is often a factor on the plateau. Pack a shell and insulating layers suitable for high-mountain weather. The Beartooths, a huge mass of high

BEARTOOTH MOUNTAINS, MT

country, are a magnet for any foul weather passing by. Do not underestimate the potential for hypothermic conditions, even in midsummer. Because of restrictions on food storage, bring a bear-resistant canister.

*GUIDE SERVICES: Both Skyline Guest Ranch and Guide Service (406-838-2380) and Sparetooth Plateau Outfitters (800-253-8545) will arrange drop camps for backpackers, while the Cooke City Bike Shack (406-838-2412) guides day-hikes only.

*GUIDEBOOKS AND MAPS: *Hiking the Absaroka and Beartooth Wilderness: A Falcon Guide*, by Bill Schneider (Globe Pequot Press, 800-243-0495, $15.95); *Beartooth Wilderness Map* (Gallatin National Forest, 406-848-7375, $6).

*CONTACT: Gardiner Ranger District, Gallatin National Forest (406-848-7375).

BIG BEND NATIONAL PARK, TEXAS

In a state full of big and bold, nothing tops the Bend

If it weren't for a stone sign announcing the park, or the summits on the horizon, Big Bend would hardly distinguish itself from the miles of Chihuahuan Desert that surround it.

But travel into the northern section of the park, and you eventually discover a land peppered with flowers, giant cacti, and mesas that will humble even the most well-traveled outdoorsman. You'll also find the Rio Grande, cradling the park to the south, and across it, the wild expanse of Old Mexico.

Once you've plunged into Big Bend, you have an 800,000-acre decision to make. You could dayhike high into the Chisos Mountains until the air grows cold with elevation and you arrive at The Window, a mountain gap and perfect natural perch for sunset watching. Or you could climb onto the South Rim, where un-Texas-like stands of maple and aspen abut steep cliffs, and the sprawling panorama spoils your eyes with its beauty.

If you want to stay grounded, head to the lip of the Santa Elena Canyon in the park's southwest, where you can watch the Rio Grande meander from 1,500 feet above. Or travel to the other side of the park and enjoy the river (not to mention historic rock art) up close while relaxing in a rustic, 105°F stone hot spring.

No matter where you go, expect to see knee-high bluebonnets and packs of free-roaming javelinas, not to mention settler-era ghost towns—reminders of this land's wild present and past.

FIELD JOURNAL

_____

_____

_____

_____

_____

_____

_____

_____

_____

_____

_____

_____

_____

_____

_____

_____

_____

_____

_____

_____

_____

Expedition Planner

*PERMITS: Pick up a free backcountry use permit from the park's visitor centers. Permits are issued in person only, on a first come, first served basis up to 24 hours before your hike. Permits for high-Chisos designated campsites are available at the Chisos Basin Visitor Center. Entrance to the park costs $15 per vehicle per week, $5 per motorcycle. A Big Bend Annual Pass is $20. You may also use your National Parks Pass or Golden Pass (Age, Eagle, and Access).

*ACCESS: Park headquarters are 70 miles south of Marathon, Texas, and 108 miles from Alpine. Three paved roads lead to the park: US 385, from Marathon to the north entrance; TX 118, from Alpine to the west entrance; and Ranch Road 170, from Presidio to Study Butte, and then TX 118 to the west entrance.

*SEASON: View wildflowers, cacti, and migrating birds from October through April. Avoid the summer, when temperatures in excess of 110°F along the Rio Grande make hiking unbearable. The rainy season usually begins in June and lasts into the fall.

*GEAR: Each hiker should carry—and drink—at least 1 gallon of water per day. Springs and *tinajas* are hard to find and may be unsafe to drink. In the desert, springs are rare and the wildlife depends on them.

*GUIDE SERVICES: Guides are available for river-related activities only. Contact Big Bend River Tours in Study Butte (800-545-4240), Desert Sports in Tel-

ringua (915-371-2727 or 888-989-6900), Rio Grande Adventures in Study Butte (915-371-2567 or 800-343-1640), or Texas River Expeditions/Far Flung in Study Butte (915-371-2633 or 800-839-7238).

*GUIDEBOOKS AND MAPS: *Hiking Big Bend National Park: A Falcon Guide by Laurence Parent*, (Globe Pequot Press, 800-243-0495, $12.95).

*CONTACT: Big Bend National Park (915-477-2251).

BOB MARSHALL WILDERNESS, MONTANA

Escape to a timeless Montana wilderness

There are plenty of ways to enter the Lower 48's fifth-largest wilderness, but none compare to Headquarters Pass. Consider this a 7,743-foot witness stand in the court of the Northern Rockies. Before you are ridges, talus piles, crumbling cliffs, and the sky, all evidence of time immemorial. And the wind greets you with a blast like a final judgment: You are little and temporary; the Bob is big, wild, and forever.

Inside these million-plus acres (which straddle the Flathead and Lewis and Clark National Forests) are trails, trails, and more trails. The most popular destination is the spectacular Chinese Wall, a thousand-foot-high reef of limestone stretching 17 miles. But for both scenery and solitude, head to the North Wall, a 13-mile-

long cliff band that's shorter than its Chinese brother but feels more rugged and primitive.

Along the roughly 6-day loop hike (starting from the east side of the wilderness), you'll wander past meadows and through clouds of grazing mountain goats. Several areas wear the scars of wildfires, with conifer saplings, bear grass, and fire-weed coloring the ground around charred husks of dead trees. When you settle in for the night, that sound you hear outside your tent is probably a family of elk clomping through your campsite. Then again, it's not un-common out here to discover fresh bear tracks in the morning. If you're feeling unsteady, it's okay to turn back. The Bob isn't going anywhere.

FIELD JOURNAL

Expedition Planner

*PERMITS: None.

*ACCESS: There are 1,100 miles of trails here and numerous ways to get in. For Headquarters Pass, take US 89 to Teton Canyon Road. Go west 17 miles, until you reach a fork. Go left and drive until the road ends.

*SEASON: The prime hiking season is from mid-June through mid-September. Those months feature sunny days and temperatures around 70°F, with occasional afternoon thunderstorms; at night, expect temperatures between 30° and 50°F. Snow starts flying in early autumn and lingers in the high passes into early summer (sometimes later after a winter of heavy snowfall).

*GEAR: Cold-weather gear is a must, as it can snow in July at high elevations. Campfires are allowed, but take a backpacker's stove in case there are fire restrictions. Also, bring a bear-resistant food canister. You'll be in bear country, after all.

*GUIDE SERVICES: High Country Adventures (406-466-5699).

*GUIDEBOOKS AND MAPS: *Hiking Montana's Bob Marshall Wilderness: A Falcon Guide*, by Erik Molvar (Globe Pequot Press, 800-243-0495, $19.95). A 1:100,000-scale contoured trail map can be purchased from Flathead National Forest (406-758-5200).

*CONTACT: Lewis and Clark National Forest (406-791-7700).

BOUNDARY WATERS CANOE AREA WILDERNESS, MINNESOTA

Dip a paddle into Minnesota's blue routes

In your dreams, a yellow ball of sun pulls itself over Pike, Caribou, and Pine Lakes through a tangle of mist dripping with light. A gull calls from somewhere off the point. The smells of camp coffee and pine needles fill the air. Once in your life, a trip should be this good, mornings this beautiful, lakes this clear, fishing this easy, and wolf tracks this fresh. In the Boundary Waters Canoe Area Wilderness, they just might be.

There are thousands of canoe routes here, but if a life-altering paddle is your hope, find the Frost River–Whipped Lake–Round Lake route. This weeklong aquatic journey is both challenging (you'll nego- tiate narrow rapids and waterfalls) and serene (there's open-lake paddling and, thanks to a couple of tough portages, real solitude). Along the way, you'll spot moose and beavers while you fish, float, and enjoy the silence.

Sometime during your journey, the vast- ness of the BWCAW may creep into your mind, and you'll flash on a thrilling truth: you're crossing a million-acre wildlife preserve, buffered from civilization by thousands of lakes, countless islands, and as many moose tracks as there are stars in the clear night sky. Then again, maybe your thoughts will stay put, focused on the calm, intimate lagoons and forest groves that immedi- ately surround you. The approaches are different, but the results don't change: you'll have an outdoors experience like none in your life before. From the minute your canoe hits ground, you'll be ready to return.

FIELD JOURNAL

_____

Expedition Planner

★PERMITS: You'll need a permit to hike or paddle in any area of the wilderness. Reservations for choice entry points fill quickly, and getting a permit can be complex, so start planning your trip 6 to 8 months in advance.

★ACCESS: The Frost River route is one of many accessed from the Gunflint Trail, northwest of Grand Marais, Minnesota. Park at the Round Lake Public Landing.

★SEASON: Spring and fall have the fewest bugs and highest water levels.

★GEAR: Standard canoeing gear, including life jackets, is a must. Raingear and a water treatment system are suggested.

★GUIDE SERVICES: Car shuttles, canoe rentals, and guide services can be arranged through many local outfitters. Call Superior National Forest (see "Contact," below) for a list.

★GUIDEBOOKS AND MAPS: *Boundary Waters Canoe Area: The Eastern Region* and *Boundary Waters Canoe Area: The Western Region*, both by Robert Beymer (Wilderness Press, 800-443-7227, $14.95 each). For the Frost River route: *Little Saganaga and Tuscarora Lakes #7* and *Knife, Kekekabic and Thomas Lakes #8* (McKenzie Maps, 800-749-2113, $5.95 each).

★CONTACT: Boundary Waters Canoe Area Wilderness, Superior National Forest (218-626-4300).

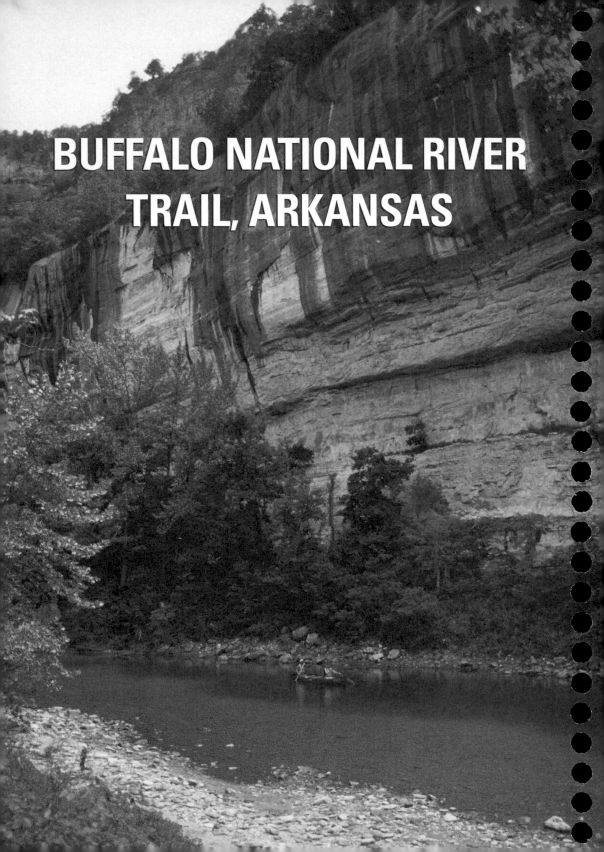

BUFFALO NATIONAL RIVER TRAIL, ARKANSAS

The river will get you high;
the trail will send you soaring

Huckleberries are fine eating anywhere, but the flavor of a Buffalo National River huckleberry will make your tongue dance. They taste of blue rock, black dirt, seeps lined with dark-green sedges, and turquoise river water. That's a lot to fit into a berry, but spend some time hiking the Buffalo National River Trail, and you'll understand. This landscape, dominated by the short, steep dips and crests of the Ozarks, soaks into the skin.

Historically, the big draw here has been the river itself, which meanders along ancient limestone bluffs. But the path, running the high ground above the river, has gained admirers and is arguably the Buffalo National River's most inspiring adventure. From the highland, the Boxley Valley vistas are long and deep; in winter, after the leaves have fallen, the cliffs and outcrops seem even more imposing. Dotting the trail are waterfalls, the remains of antebellum farmhouses, and shelters once occupied by Native Americans. Caroline silver bells and jacks-in-the-pulpit rock steadily in the trailside wind, scattered among other wildflowers, sweet gums, and giant beeches.

Today, the Buffalo National River Trail is divided into two sections, which may eventually be combined to stretch 100 miles. In some plans, the trail will link Arkansas's Ozark Highlands Trail and Missouri's Ozark Trail to form a nearly 1,000-mile system, sure to become one of the great challenges of the Southeast. For now, trek from Ponca to the Pruitt trailhead, a 3-day, 26-mile stretch, and whet your appetite for the Buffalo to come.

FIELD JOURNAL

BUFFALO NATIONAL RIVER TRAIL, AR

Expedition Planner

★PERMITS: No permits are necessary to hike the trail or canoe the Buffalo National River. Campsites are available on a first come, first served basis, and fees vary by location. Call (870) 449-4311 or (870) 439-2502 for reservations.

★ACCESS: The trailhead at Ponca is 154 miles (about 3 hours) northwest of Little Rock, Arkansas. The Ponca trailhead is 1 mile south of Ponca on AR 43. To start in Boxley, take AR 21 through Harrison, Arkansas, and continue south for 43 miles. The Boxley trailhead is on the right; you can park right there.

★SEASON: With the region's mild winters, you can hike the Buffalo National River Trail year-round. Late spring can be wet (bring raingear), and summer humid.

The best hikes are in early spring, after the wildflowers begin blooming but before the leaves clutter the view, and early fall, when the turning leaves *are* the view. You'll avoid snakes (copperheads, water moccasins, and rattlesnakes), bugs, and heat in either of these two seasons. This is the only national park in the Lower 48 that allows hunting, from early fall to late spring. Be aware, but not wary.

★**GEAR:** No special gear is needed.

★**GUIDE SERVICES:** Guides are not available for hiking.

★**GUIDEBOOKS AND MAPS:** *Buffalo River Hiking Trails* (Cloudland.net, 800-838-4453, $18.95).

★**CONTACT:** Buffalo National River, Tyler Bend Ranger Station (870-439-2502).

CANYONLANDS
NATIONAL PARK, UTAH

Find yourself among the lost canyons of Utah

Rock, water, and air: In southern Utah's Canyonlands National Park, it seems there's nothing else. The land rises in haphazard skyscrapers, iron striped, dusty white, and brown against the neon sky. Buttes pocked with watery potholes sit near mesas streaked with desert varnish. Boulders spill riotously into deep slices of earth. The cool wind here may be the only reminder that these desert environs are thousands of feet above the sea. And through it all, the Colorado and Green Rivers run, colliding in a water-and-stone spectacular known as The Confluence.

The rivers divide the park into three sections, each promising distinct Western landscapes. The Needles lies to the east in a mass of sandstone and pillars. Island in the Sky is a 6,000-foot-high mesa towering 1,000 feet over the terrain, with 850-mile views on a good day. But the rock may be most outrageous in the park's remote Maze district, a favorite stomping ground of solitude seekers like *The Monkey Wrench Gang* scribe Edward Abbey. Take the 15-mile North Trail Canyon to the Maze Overlook, then drop down to explore the otherworldly spiderweb of canyons. Be aware, though: Getting lost during your hunt for world-class rock art, pictographs, and petroglyphs from 1,000 B.C. could cost you hours in dead ends. They don't call it the Maze for nothing.

FIELD JOURNAL

Expedition Planner

★PERMITS: Backpacking permits ($15 for 14 days) are required for overnight trips. All permits may be reserved at least 2 weeks in advance (435-259-4351). Backpackers can stay for up to 7 consecutive nights in any site or zone. Park entry costs $5 per person for 7 days, or $10 per vehicle for 7 days. You may also use your National Parks Pass or Golden Pass (Age, Eagle, and Access).

★ACCESS: For Island in the Sky: Take US 191 to UT 313; follow UT 313 southwest for 22 miles to the visitor center. For Needles: From US 191, take UT 211 west for 35 miles to the visitor center. For the Maze: Take I-70 to UT 24 south; follow UT 24 for 42 miles. After Goblin Valley State Park, turn left onto a dirt road. Follow this for 45 miles to the Hans Flat Ranger Station.

★SEASON: Spring, with its blooming flowers and more plentiful water sources, is more popular than the other ideal hiking season, fall.

*GEAR: Clean water is hard to find in the park, and temperatures can get very hot; pack and drink at least a gallon of drinking water for each day, and check spring conditions with a ranger station before you set out. Even though it's a desert, bring raingear. The park forbids hikers from burning or burying toilet paper, so bring plastic bags to pack it out. Also, bring or rent a bear-resistant container to protect food from rodents.

*GUIDE SERVICES: Call the park for a list of guides based in Moab (see "Contact," below).

*GUIDEBOOKS AND MAPS: *Exploring Canyonlands and Arches National Parks: A Falcon Guide*, by Bill Schneider (Globe Pequot Press, 800-243-0495, $14.95); *Canyonlands National Park #246 and #210* (National Geographic Trails Illustrated Maps, 800-962-1643, $9.95).

*CONTACT: Canyonlands National Park (435-719-2100).

CATSKILL MOUNTAINS, NEW YORK

Picture-pretty hiking in the wilds of the Northeast

On the Catskill Mountains Escarpment Trail, which rides a thin lip of stone above the picturesque Hudson River Valley, you can truly say the hikes are works of art. Rip Van Winkle Hollow, at the south end of the trail, is where, legend holds, the drowsy Dutchman dozed undisturbed for 20 years. And Artists and Sunset Rocks, above North Lake—also along the Escarpment—are where 19th-century artists Thomas Cole, Frederic Edwin Church, and other Hudson River School painters found inspiration for masterworks that now hang in the world's leading museums.

But from a hiker's perspective, the real artistry behind the 23-mile Escarpment is the sustained ridgeline walking and ever-changing scenery: mixed hardwood forests, dark hemlock groves beside swift-flowing creeks, hardscrabble-pitch pine at southern-facing outcrops, and a spruce-fir cap on the higher peaks.

The only price to access this woodland museum is paid in muscle and sweat. The soft sediments underlying these ancient mountains were carved vengefully by glaciers some 22,000 years ago, creating topographical changes both sudden and steep. Around here, it's not the elevation extremes that count; it's the ups and downs in between.

Allow yourself time to indulge temptation and sidetrack across the Blackhead Mountains to summit Black Dome and Thomas Cole Mountain. You'll be able to make out the southern Adirondacks and Green Mountains, the Berkshires and Taconics, the Hudson Highlands around West Point, and the chalky-white Shawangunks. At moments like these, life exceeds art.

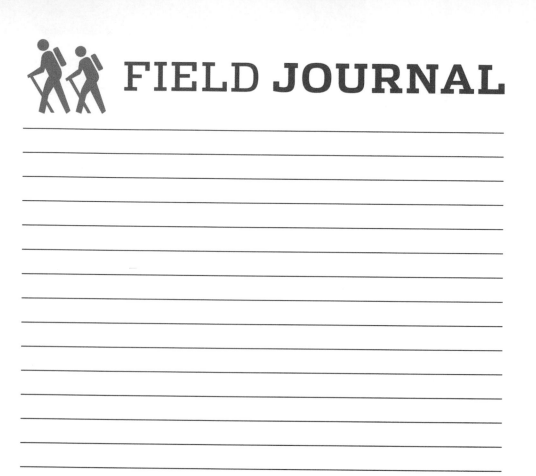

FIELD JOURNAL

Expedition Planner

★PERMITS: If you're camping on state land for more than 3 nights, you'll need a free permit from the local forest ranger. Call the New York State Department of Environmental Conservation (see "Contact," opposite page) to find the nearest station.

★ACCESS: The southern trailhead for the Escarpment Trail in the Catskill Forest Preserve is 120 miles (2 hours) north of New York City. From exit 20 (Saugerties) off I-87, follow NY 32A north to Palenville. When you reach the town, pick up NY 23A west, and follow it through scenic Kaaterskill Clove. Turn right onto North Lake Road (NY 18), in the hamlet of Haines Falls. Just before the campground entrance, turn right onto Schutt Road. Trailhead parking is on the right.

★SEASON: Fall leaf-peeping season typically peaks around Columbus Day, but skip the gazing crowds and hike here during the rest of the year instead. See bald eagles in winter and wildflowers come summer.

_____

_____

_____

_____

_____

_____

_____

_____

_____

_____

_____

_____

_____

_____

_____

_____

_____

_____

_____

_____

GEAR: Although the Catskills provide New York City with 90 percent of its drinking water, most hikers don't know which streams are pure, so bring water treatment supplies. Remember snowshoes in winter and crampons in early spring to traverse the packed-down snow and ice.

GUIDE SERVICES: Aaron Bennett of the Catskill Center for Conservation and Development (845-254-9977) leads private hikes.

GUIDEBOOKS AND MAPS: *Catskill Mountain Guide: Hiking Trails in the Catskills*, by Peter Kick (Appalachian Mountain Club Books, 800-262-4455, $19.95); *Catskill Trails* five-map set (New York–New Jersey Trail Conference, 201-512-9348, $13.95).

CONTACT: New York State Department of Environmental Conservation, Region 4 (607-652-7365).

CEDAR MESA,
UTAH

Disappear into the oldest Old West

The lure of prehistoric ruins isn't the only reason to hike into Cedar Mesa. The weather-worn slickrock, towering stone amphitheaters, spring-fed gardens, and awesome silence of this sandstone maze are attraction enough.

Still, it must be said: Without its artifacts, Cedar Mesa would be just another slice of spectacular canyon country. Here is your chance to walk and camp among signs of one of the world's most mysterious vanishing acts. For centuries, Native Americans built cliff dwellings and granaries in this complex of steep-walled canyons. They carved rock drawings—petroglyphs and pictographs—in sandstone faces,

leaving countless panels of spellbinding, indecipherable art. They crafted pottery, arrowheads, and sandals. Then, 800 years ago, they departed—seemingly overnight.

Today, Cedar Mesa stands as one of the original American ghost towns—a place so rife with Anasazi and other Native American relics that local rangers are compelled to remind prospective visitors to behave respectfully, asking, "Would you want someone violating your ancestors' bones?" You may not see the burial sites and ruins at first, but you can be certain the spirits of the past are here, maybe even right under your feet. (Literally. Watch the ground carefully, lest you stumble through the hidden roof into an 800-year-old kiva.) Bring plenty of film, but don't even think about souvenirs: All archeological remains are protected by federal law.

Though there are few official trails on Cedar Mesa, the most popular routes in the Grand Gulch area are well trod. For more adventurous exploring, get a map, tank up on water, and chart your own course into the past.

FIELD JOURNAL

CEDAR MESA, UT

Expedition Planner

*PERMITS: Backcountry permits are required for hiking in nearly all Cedar Mesa canyons. Reservations are available for spring and fall, with a limited number of walk-in permits issued at Kane Gulch Ranger Station. Between March 1 and June 14, and between September 1 and October 31, permits are $8 per person per trip. The rest of the year, permits are $5 per person per trip.

*ACCESS: Trailheads for most Cedar Mesa canyons are accessed off UT 261 in southeastern Utah. Stop first at Kane Gulch Ranger Station, 4 miles south of UT 95 on UT 261, to pick up your backcountry permit.

★**SEASON:** Spring and fall offer the best weather but also the most competition for permits. Winter can be bitter cold, and summer sizzling hot.

★**GEAR:** Bring a hydration pack or extra bottles of water, plus an umbrella for shade during the day.

★**GUIDE SERVICES:** Contact the ranger (see "Contact," at right) for a list of guides.

★**GUIDEBOOKS AND MAPS:** *A Hiking Guide to Cedar Mesa: Southeast Utah*, by Peter Francis Tassoni (University of Utah Press, 800-773-6672, $19.95); *Grand Gulch Plateau #706* (National Geographic Trails Illustrated Maps, 800-962-1643, $9.95).

★**CONTACT:** Bureau of Land Management, Monticello Field Office (435-587-1532).

CONTINENTAL DIVIDE TRAIL

Go high and go long on the Rocky Mountain trail of trails

Of all the long trails in the United States, there are none higher than the Continental Divide Trail. At 3,100 miles, this primitive, rugged backcountry skywalk starts at the U.S.-Canada border and doesn't stop until it hits Mexico.

In between, you'll find five huge Western states, 25 national forests, 20 wilderness areas, eight Bureau of Land Management resource areas, three national parks, and one national monument. And you'll do it all—or most of it, anyway—in the Rocky Mountain high terrain, along a route that, at sections, exists only on paper. By comparison, the Appalachian and Pacific Crest feel like starter trails.

Only about two-dozen people un-

dertake the entire CDT every year. All other visitors seek out one of its hundreds of access points for dayhikes or backpacking trips. The best of the best is the trail from Stony Pass to Wolf Creek Pass in Colorado's Weminuche Wilderness, one of the longest and highest wilderness stretches of the CDT. You'll trek 95 miles of skyscraping country, crossing only one road and rarely dipping below 12,000 feet.

If you're closer to Canada, visit the section that traverses western Montana's 159,086-acre Anaconda-Pintler Wilderness, in the Bitterroot and Beaverhead-Deerlodge National Forests. Here, the peaks top 10,000 feet; the landscape offers constant classic-Rockies panoramas of bare rock, craggy peaks, and alpine lakes; and the mountain goats, cougars, elk, moose, deer, wolverines, and black bears thrive.

FIELD JOURNAL

Expedition Planner

★PERMITS: Permits are required along some sections of the CDT. Inquire with the appropriate land-management agency.

★ACCESS: Access varies along the CDT's length. There are numerous trailheads for dayhikes and for backpacking trips of virtually any distance and duration.

★SEASON: The prime hiking season varies with latitude and elevation but generally doesn't begin until early July and concludes by mid-September.

★GEAR: None.

★GUIDE SERVICES: None.

★GUIDEBOOKS AND MAPS: Four guidebooks cover the entire CDT: *Montana and Idaho's Continental Divide Trail: The Official Guide*, by Lynna and Leland Howard ($27.95); *Wyoming's Continental Divide Trail: The Official Guide*, by Lora Davis; *Colorado's Continental Divide Trail: The Official Guide*, by Tom Lorang Jones and John Fielder; and *New Mexico's Continental Divide Trail: The Official Guide*, by Bob Julyan and Tom Till. All four titles are from Westcliffe Publishers (303-935-0900); the last three are $24.95 each.

★CONTACT: Continental Divide Trail Alliance (888-909-2382).

DENALI NATIONAL PARK
AND PRESERVE, ALASKA

There's nothing like backpacking around The Big One

It is, quite simply, the most spectacular moment in North American hiking. For 3 days, the world has been locked in a gray haze of rain and fog. Mosquitoes buzz incessantly in your rain hood. You trudge along, gazing only at your feet. Finally you look up, and there it is. The clouds have cleared over the highest mountain on the continent: Mount McKinley. If the Greek gods decided to move to Alaska, surely their new Mount Olympus would look something like this.

Denali National Park and Preserve (the mountain is still officially Mount McKinley) is classic Alaska—open horizons, grizzlies, snowcapped peaks, wind swirling across the tundra. Even without Mount McKinley, it would be one of the world's premier hiking locations. But when the mountain peeks out from behind the clouds, backpacking here is simply sublime.

At 6 million acres, the park is the size of Massachusetts, but it features only one maintained backpacking trail, the McKinley-Barr. The best routes are along rivers and ridgelines and require good map-reading skills, experience in fording fast, cold streams, and the ability to keep one eye peeled for grizzlies. You won't make a lot of miles in Denali, either. The open tundra and long horizons can sometimes seem endless, as if you're getting nowhere. Then again, you can always just sit down and wait for the mountain to show itself.

FIELD JOURNAL

Expedition Planner

★PERMITS: Each of the park's back-country units has a user quota that fills quickly in the high season. Reservations cannot be made in advance, so have second and third route choices in mind.

★ACCESS: The only park entrance is off George Parks Highway, 237 miles north of Anchorage and reachable by car, shuttle, or Alaska Railroad (800-544-0552). Private cars are allowed only 15 miles into the park. Buses shuttle visitors farther along the narrow Park Road.

★SEASON: Ideal hiking is in July and August. Early September is prime berry-picking and bear-viewing time, but snow starts around Labor Day.

★GEAR: Bear-resistant food containers are required but are loaned for free with a backcountry permit purchase. Bring raingear, extra shoes for wading through rivers, headnets, and insect repellant.

★GUIDE SERVICES: Several companies are licensed to lead trips into Denali. Try Earthsong Lodge (907-683-2863).

★GUIDEBOOKS AND MAPS: *Denali National Park & Preserve, AK: Backcountry Companion*, by Jon Nierenberg (Alaska Natural History Association, 907-274-8440, $8.95); *Denali National Park #222* (National Geographic Trails Illustrated Maps, 800-962-1643, $9.95).

★CONTACT: Denali National Park and Preserve (907-683-2294).

EVERGLADES
NATIONAL PARK, FLORIDA

The Sunshine State's wettest, wildest ride

Ever backpacked on a river? Hike the 15-mile round-trip Coastal Prairie Trail in southernmost Everglades National Park, and you will. Dubbed the River of Grass, this massive ecosystem literally rests atop a torrent of water flowing imperceptibly from Lake Okeechobee in the center of the state to the Gulf of Mexico. The path is dry and your boots won't get wet (unless an alligator runs you off the trail), but surrounding you are swamps, sloughs, estuaries, and saw grass prairie—all reminders that you're in a world of water.

It's also a world of wildlife. This trail follows a makeshift road once used by fishermen and workers picking wild cotton. Just as they did, you'll penetrate shady buttonwood thickets, walk alongside mangrove-fringed lakes, and roll through wide, grassy plains. A shuffle in the brush could reveal any of 100 birds—most likely herons, hawks, bald eagles, egrets, pelicans, cormorants, ibis, ospreys, or roseate spoonbills. Or maybe it's an endangered Florida Bay crocodile—a lucky or unlucky encounter, depending on how easily you scare.

Ramble on, and you may find the mother of all sunsets at Clubhouse Beach, a wild spit of sand about as far south as you can hike and still be in Florida. Close your eyes, and you'll think you're in Tahiti. At night, without the glare of Miami lights in the sky, the stars put on quite a show. And while the bellowing mating calls of the gators may not exactly lull you to sleep, they do make for unique bedtime listening.

FIELD JOURNAL

Expedition Planner

*PERMITS: Backcountry permits, required for camping, may be obtained in person up to a day before you start your trip. Call the Flamingo Visitor Center (239-695-2945). Camping is $14 per day at the campgrounds; reserve a spot through the National Park Reservation Service (800-365-2267 or 301-722-1257) from November 1 to April 30. Entry at the main gate costs $10 per vehicle for 7 days; entry at Shark Valley costs $8 per vehicle for 7 days. There is no entrance fee at the Gulf Coast entrance. An Everglades National Park Annual Pass is $20. You can also use your National Parks Pass or Golden Pass (Age, Eagle, and Access) for entry.

*ACCESS: Drive to the Flamingo Visitor Center, 38 miles southwest of the main entrance, at the southern end of the park. Drive 1 mile past the visitor center to the Flamingo Campground. The Coastal Prairie Trail starts at the very back of Loop C. The trail will split after ⅕ of a mile. Stay to the right.

*SEASON: The period from November through April is the most pleasant time for hiking. The wet season begins in May, bringing mosquitoes, no-see-ums, and other biting insects. Hurricane season runs from June through November.

*GEAR: Tent with insect netting and a headnet to keep out pesky bugs. Carry fresh water (1 gallon per person per day), as water sources are hard to find inside the park.

*GUIDE SERVICES: For boat tours, contact Flamingo Lodge Boat Tours (941-695-3101), Everglades National Park Boat Tours (941-695-2591), or Tram Tours at Shark Valley (305-221-8455).

*GUIDEBOOKS AND MAPS: *Hidden Florida Keys and Everglades 7th Edition, Including Key Largo and Key West*, by Ann Boese and Candace Leslie (Ulysses Press, 510-601-8301, $10.36). Free maps are available at the visitor center.

*CONTACT: Everglades National Park (305-242-7700).

GATES OF THE ARCTIC NATIONAL PARK, ALASKA

Wander through wilderness the guidebook writers still haven't found

At 8.5 million acres, Gates of the Arctic is a de facto wilderness state. Here, backpacking is reduced to its most essential elements. There are no safety nets. There are no rangers (none you'll see, anyway). There are no signs and no campgrounds, no other humans. Just you and your group among the homogeneity of endless plateaus, endless valleys, endless crags of naked gray limestone. The only trails belong to the caribou.

Getting swallowed by nature stirs feral instincts. The smallest change piques the senses—flickers of movement, subtle variations of terrain, the angle of the sun. The only sound you hear for miles may be the swirl of a

river in a canyon below, tinted the bright, surreal blue of water in a dream. Slip and fall 1,000 feet, and only the ravens will know.

Even a place this untamed has popular routes, including a path through the granite spires of the Arrigetch Peaks. Some visitors head to the nearby Brooks Range, the northernmost mountain range in the United States, which features such peaks as the 8,510-foot Mount Igikpak. Others follow the streams along the North Fork of the Koyukuk River, working their way from Summit Lake down through the pair of swooping peaks (Frigid Crags, 5,501 feet; and Boreal Mountain, 6,654 feet) that form the park's eponymous "gates."

But you weren't drawn to Gates of the Arctic by famous or fashionable hikes. If you're ready for this park, you're ready for virgin terrain. Just pick a point on the map. Then go.

FIELD JOURNAL

_____

_____

_____

_____

_____

_____

_____

_____

_____

_____

_____

_____

_____

_____

_____

_____

_____

_____

_____

Expedition Planner

★PERMITS: Permits are not required, though you will need to check in at a ranger station and file a trip plan. The rangers encourage hikers to attend a safety orientation, which they offer in the nearby towns of Anaktuvuk Pass, Bettles, Coldfoot, and Kotzebue.

★ACCESS: There are no roads into the park. Take a scheduled flight to Bettles or Anaktuvuk Pass, then charter a floatplane to drop you into and pick you up from the park. Be prepared to spend extra time in the backcountry. Though you should arrive at your pickup spot well before you told the air taxi to come back for you, your pilot may be late because of bad weather. Contact the park ranger for a list of companies licensed to bring people into the park.

★SEASON: For more daylight and warmer weather, head north between late May and early September. For round-the-clock daylight, plan your trip around the summer solstice.

★GEAR: There are some glaciated areas, but an ice axe and crampons aren't necessary for most trips. You will likely need to ford streams and rivers, however, and the water here is cold. Be familiar with how to cross safely, and make sure to keep a set of clothes where it can't get wet. Carry a stove, as there's not much of a wood supply in most of the park. Bears are in good supply, though, so know how to prevent them from getting into your food; bear-resistant food canisters are strongly recommended.

★GUIDE SERVICES: Twenty-two professional guides are available. Contact a ranger for an official list (see "Contact," below).

★GUIDEBOOKS AND MAPS: Be sure to consult topographic maps. Gates is so big that it's hard to recommend any single map.

★CONTACT: Gates of the Arctic National Park and Preserve (907-457-5752).

GLACIER NATIONAL PARK, MONTANA

Find beauty in the land of the lost ice

Don't be misled by the name: Glacier National Park is many things, but it's hardly a haven for glaciers. Ages ago, the crystalline giants slunk through here, inching their way toward sea level. Today, the great glaciers are merely ice cubes, blankly occupying the park's north-facing cirques.

If Glacier's frozen patches disappoint, however, you can always turn to the footprints the ice caps left behind. The park is awash in U-shaped valleys, castle-like peaks, shorn cliffs, and emerald tarns. Where clumpets once thawed, lilies now thrive. Where floes blocked the path, backpackers move freely.

Make that very freely. Nearly 730 miles of trails weave in, out, and around the ledges and lagoons here, taking you past an array of flora and fauna of the wildest variety. A single outing might find surefooted mountain goats, moose, elk, and wolverines within a mile or two of each other. To take full advantage of the glaciers' demise, hike the 6-day, 58-mile Great Northern Traverse from Belly River to Kintla Lake. You'll start out among a stunning array of wildflowers, including glacier lilies and Indian paintbrush. Along the way, you'll pass stair-stepped waterfalls, sacred Native American sites, a 120-foot suspension bridge, and 90-mile prairie views. And at Kintla, the rippling remnant of those extinct glaciers will sit glassy among the trees, reflecting the mountains and sky above. Frozen or not, the scenery will give you chills.

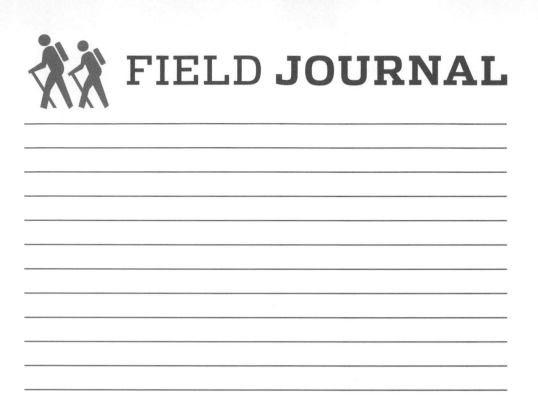

FIELD JOURNAL

Expedition Planner

★PERMITS: Driving into the park costs $10 for 7 days or $20 for an annual pass. You can also use your National Parks Pass or Golden Pass (Age, Eagle, and Access) for entry. If reserved in advance, the required backcountry use permits are $4 a night per person age 16 and older, plus a $20 processing fee. More than one-fourth of the campsites can be reserved. You can pick up a walk-in permit within the 24 hours before the start of your hike.

★ACCESS: Fly into Glacier Park International Airport in Kalispell, Montana, 25 miles from West Glacier, or into Great Falls, Montana, 200 miles from West Glacier. You can rent a car at either airport or hire a shuttle from the airport in Kalispell. The park prohibits vehicles longer than 21 feet or wider than 8 feet from traveling the steepest sections of Going-to-the-Sun Road. To get to the Great Northern Traverse, take US 2 to US 89 north. Drive for almost 50 miles. You'll pass the park's main entrance in St. Mary. Turn left onto MT 17, and follow this west for 15 miles to Chief Mountain customs, where you can park your car. Leave another car at Kintla Lake, as no shuttle service is available there.

★SEASON: Snow generally limits high-country hiking to the period from July through September.

★GEAR: Carry bear spray. If you're hiking in late spring, bring an ice axe and crampons, and be aware of the possibility of snowstorms, avalanches, and other water hazards. It snows every month on the peaks. Even if you're going to Glacier in July, bring cold-weather gear.

★GUIDE SERVICES: Glacier Wilderness Guides (800-521-7238), out of West Glacier, is the only licensed backpacking guide service in Glacier National Park.

★GUIDEBOOKS AND MAPS: *Hiking Glacier and Waterton Lakes National Parks: A Falcon Guide*, by Eric Molvar (Globe Pequot Press, 800-243-0495, $14.95); *Glacier/Waterton Lakes National Parks #215* (National Geographic Trails Illustrated Maps, 800-962-1643, $9.95).

★CONTACT: Glacier National Park (406-888-7800).

GRAND CANYON
NATIONAL PARK, ARIZONA

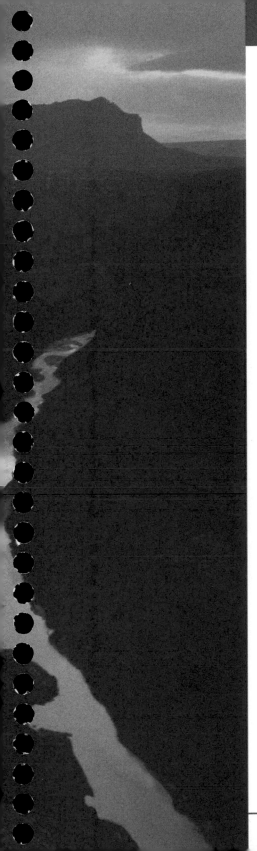

Hike through geologic time to find ancient, hidden treasures

A mile deep. Seventy-one thousand foot-steps wide. Some 277 miles long, as the river flows. Nearly 2 billion years of exposed geologic history—more than anyplace else on Earth. The statistics for Arizona's Grand Canyon are impressive, but reading them won't change your perspective with the same explosive force as a hike into the heart of this otherworldly natural wonder.

The tallest man alive is but a grain of sand in this ancient, gargantuan landscape. To see what we mean, hike the 10 miles down from the canyon's South Rim to the Colorado River along the Tanner Trail: You lose 5,000 feet of elevation and all sense of scale along the way. In the Grand Canyon, landmarks that seem nearby actually stand 2 or 5 or 20 miles away. Layers of earth, not the hands on your watch, mark the passage of time. Light reflects off rock, making every color radiate with a neon glow.

For a hard but heavenly trek, thread your way between boulders and sheer bluffs, following the faintly marked Escalante Route, on the eastern end of the Tonto Trail. Lush riverside campsites await, where soft sand and abundant water make you forget you're in the desert. But in between, the route scrambles up scree slopes 1,000 feet above the river, detours around serpentine drainages, and slides down narrow canyons. You'll wipe a lot of sweat from your brow and leave feeling smaller than ever before.

It's a small price to pay to feel so alive.

FIELD JOURNAL

_____
_____
_____
_____
_____
_____
_____
_____
_____
_____
_____
_____
_____
_____
_____
_____
_____
_____
_____
_____
_____
_____

Expedition Planner

★PERMITS: Permits are required for all overnight camping. Get one 4 months in advance by mailing a request to Backcountry Office, Grand Canyon National Park, PO Box 129, Grand Canyon, AR 86023, or faxing it to (928) 638-2125. You can also apply for a same-day permit at the park's backcountry office, but demand often exceeds supply. Fees are $10 per group, plus $5 per person per night of camping.

★ACCESS: Fly into Grand Canyon Airport, or drive from Phoenix or Las Vegas. There are also flights into Flagstaff, Arizona. Once you reach the park, use the Tanner Trail, at Lipan Point near Desert View, or the New Hance Trail, near Moran Point, to access the Escalante Trail.

★SEASON: Spring and late fall are the most pleasant times to hike. In winter, be prepared for ice and snow at the rim. Do not backpack here from June to early September—temperatures can soar to 115°F at the base of the canyon.

★GEAR: Bring as little as possible. In spring and fall, you may not even need a tent or sleeping bag. Make sure to bring plenty of food and water; the latter should take up most of the room in your pack. Fires are not allowed, so bring a stove.

★GUIDE SERVICES: Many are available. For day or overnight hikes, contact Grand Canyon Hikes (928-779-1615), High Sonoran Adventures (480-614-3331), or Sky Island Treks (520-622-6966).

★GUIDEBOOKS AND MAPS: *Hiking the Grand Canyon*, by John Annerino (Sierra Club Books, 415-977-5500, $15); *Grand Canyon National Park #207* (National Geographic Trails Illustrated Maps, 800-962-1643, $9.95). U.S. Geological Surveys exist for the Escalante Route: Desert View, Cape Royal, and Grandview Point (USGS, 888-ASK-USGS, $6 each).

★CONTACT: Backcountry Information Center, Grand Canyon National Park (928-638-7875).

GRAND TETON NATIONAL PARK, WYOMING

Feast your eyes on North America's most stunning mountain range

The wildlife is spectacular, but an honest hiker will admit to coming here for the peaks. The jagged Teton Range thrusts up from the valley around Jackson Hole, offering a dozen steep spires above 12,000 feet. The masterstroke of this living mural is Grand Teton itself, rising above the canyon headwall like a shark's fin knifing through ocean swells. At its side, the jagged pyramid of Mount Owen cuts a brooding silhouette. It's a skyline to stop you in your tracks, no matter how many times you visit.

The 38-mile Teton Crest Trail, a sustained high-country hike with

campsites and killer views, squeezes this scenery for all it's worth. It's a classic-Teton, serpentine, alpine path that seldom dips below 8,000 feet. You'll pass bold limestone outcrops amid forget-me-nots, gerbil-like pikas, and the occasional shadow of a golden eagle flying overhead. Eventually, you'll drop into a stunted conifer forest and then make your way down to Marion Lake, which glows green in the midday sun. At Death Canyon Shelf, you'll get your first view of the Tetons across a field of wildflowers. You may want to stop here and gaze in awe, but there's more ahead: By the time you surmount Hurricane Pass, where the distant Grand Teton seems close enough to touch, you'll have entered a high-country hiking trance from which you may never return.

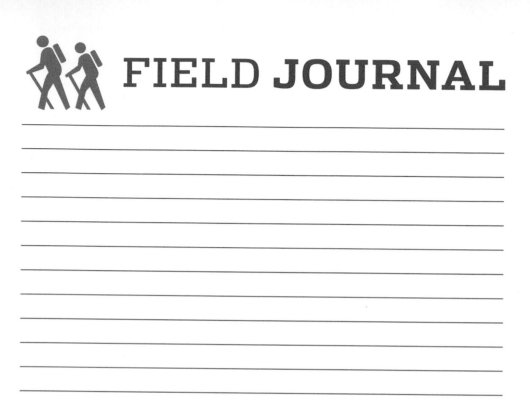

FIELD JOURNAL

_____

_____

_____

_____

_____

_____

_____

_____

_____

_____

_____

_____

_____

_____

_____

_____

_____

_____

_____

_____

_____

_____

Expedition Planner

★PERMITS: Pick up a free backcountry use permit from Moose or Colter Bay Visitor Centers or Jenny Lake Ranger Station within the 24 hours before the start of your hike. Two-thirds of the permits are handed out on a first come, first served basis. The rest may be reserved from January 1 to May 15 for $15. Park passes, good for both Grand Teton and Yellowstone, are $20 for 7 days or $40 for the year. You can also use your National Parks Pass or Golden Pass (Age, Eagle, and Access) for entry.

★ACCESS: If you're driving from Jackson Hole Airport, follow US 89 south into the town of Jackson and turn right onto WY 22. Follow this for about 7 miles, then turn right onto WY 390 (also called Village Road). After 5 miles, turn left into Teton Village. The Jackson Hole Aerial Tram (307-733-2292) will be right in front of you. For $15 to $17, you can ride 4,139 feet up to the 10,450-foot summit of Rendezvous Mountain. The tram operates from the end of May to mid-September.

★SEASON: With only 60 frost-free days, the park is ideal for hiking from mid-July through mid-September. Most of the trails are melted out by July and don't see new snow until at least September. If it's been a snowy winter, however, Paintbrush Canyon may retain a snowfield through July.

*GEAR: An ice axe might not be necessary, but it's a good idea to bring one and know how to use it. The canyon supports black bears, so bring bear canisters and bear spray. The trails in the Grand Teton National Park system are fairly rocky, so bring sturdy hiking boots. And the weather here, as in many mountain parks, is unpredictable. There are thunderstorms on the warmest, sunniest July days. Bring raingear.

*GUIDE SERVICES: None. Though the park does not allow any company to give tours of the area, rangers do lead nature walks and short dayhikes.

*GUIDEBOOKS AND MAPS: Hiking Grand Teton National Park: A Falcon Guide, by Bill Schneider (Globe Pequot Press, 800-243-0495, $12.95); Grand Teton National Park #202 (National Geographic Trails Illustrated Maps, 800-962-1643, $9.95).

*CONTACT: Grand Teton National Park (307-739-3399).

GREAT SMOKY MOUNTAINS NATIONAL PARK, NORTH CAROLINA/ TENNESSEE

The hills are alive with fog and flowers

The name says it all. This is a land where the mountains breathe, where blue mist haunts the grass lines and weaves among the trees. These are the crests that speak of regeneration, of 300 million years of growth and erosion. Here, the wet-smelling flowers or lush vegetation you find off-trail may be an undiscovered species. Life is as big as it can be.

Is it any wonder, then, that Great Smoky Mountains National Park attracts 10 million visitors each year—more than any other national park in the United States? (By comparison, the Grand Canyon draws 3 million.) A hike under these old-growth hemlock and tulip trees, where the sunlight is content to drop through in ribbons, will draw superlatives from even the most taciturn outdoorsman. Rugged 6,000-foot peaks, crazy coves of Carolina silver bells and magnolias, spruce and fir, beech, birch, and maple pack Great Smoky's 800 square miles, in celebration of the North Carolina–Tennessee border.

To wring the most out of Great Smoky, try the hike through Gregory and Parson Balds. This 15.6-mile loop will send you scrambling over the steep, dry reaches along the Wolf Ridge and Long Hungry Ridge trails. You'll be rewarded when you reach the balds—rare high openings in the canopy which, in early summer, are covered by row upon row of flaming azaleas and rhododendron blossoms. Take a tip from the Smokies here and sit still, breathing deeply and bathing in nature.

FIELD JOURNAL

Expedition Planner

★PERMITS: A free permit is required for backcountry camping; obtain one from the visitor center (see "Contact," below). There's no entrance fee. For a mile-high campsite, head to Sheep Pen Gap, nestled between the two balds. You'll need reservations (865-436-1231), especially during the ever-popular June blooming season.

★ACCESS: The park is located 190 miles north of Atlanta and 227 miles west of Charlotte, North Carolina. The trailhead to Gregory and Parson Balds is at Twentymile Ranger Station, 5 miles west of Fontana Village on NC 28. To get to Wolf Ridge Trail, you'll first hike ½ mile on Twentymile Trail.

★SEASON: You can hike here year-round. To avoid the crowds, don't go in October, which is the busiest time, or from June through August.

★GEAR: As they say in eastern Tennessee, if you don't like the weather, wait 5 minutes. The weather is highly unpredictable in the mountains, so dress in layers and bring raingear.

★GUIDE SERVICES: A Walk in the Woods (865-436-8283) and Outdoor Adventures (865-774-5885) offer interpretive hikes, as do the rangers.

★GUIDEBOOKS AND MAPS: *Great Smoky Mountains National Park Destination Guide* (National Geographic Trails Illustrated Maps, 800-962-1643, $11.95).

★CONTACT: Great Smoky Mountains National Park Visitor Center (865-436-1291 [days] or 865-436-1200 [nights]).

INCA TRAIL, PERU

The road to Machu Picchu is lined with stunning visions

Many visitors to southern Peru make it to the archeological marvel that is Machu Picchu. But only the privileged—those strong of mind and leg—brave the original mountain-hiking route of the city's former residents. Hikes like this are the reason men backpack.

From the moment you get off the train out of Cuzco and begin your 4-day, 26-mile hike into the thin air of the Andes Mountains, you'll encounter wonders straight out of ancient Peru. You'll climb up and down ancient stone steps that wind through the mountains, lifting you toward mind-altering views of the region's towering crests, tropical flora, and the South American sky. Along the way, you'll see the Incan stonework that makes this a hike apart, including aqueducts, baths, tiers, and tunnels that the Incas dug through solid stone. These ruins are your reward for taking this route to Machu Picchu instead of riding the train to one of several closer depots.

Finally, a notch in the hillside known as the Gateway of the Sun reveals the complex at Machu Picchu fanned out on the terraced ridge below. As you enter, you may find tourists who swept in by train, posing for photographs and laughing at their good fortune in reaching these ruins. Here, you'll attempt the greatest of all Inca Trail challenges: smiling politely and suppressing the urge to boast.

FIELD JOURNAL

Expedition Planner

★PERMITS: The Peruvian government has recently tightened restrictions on visiting the ruins. Five hundred people may begin the trail each day, and each hiker must be with a licensed guide and group (maximum group size is 16 people). You will need a permit, but your guide will take care of this for your group.

★ACCESS: Fly to Lima, connect to Cuzco, then take the train from Cuzco to Aguas Calientes. Depart at kilometer 88, at Qorihuayrachina near Ollantaytambo. After your hike, you can return to Cuzco on the economy train, known as the Backpacker.

★SEASON: The dry season, from June through September, brings more tourists and optimal hiking. Try going in May for fewer people. Avoid July 28 through August 10, when the site is crowded for national holidays.

★GEAR: No special gear is needed.

★GUIDE SERVICES: Buy packages only from licensed companies, such as U.S.-based Wilderness Travel (800-368-2794) or Peru's Inca Explorers (011-51-84-241-070) or United Mice (011-51-84-221-139). Many hikers buy packages before leaving for Peru, though it's possible to hire a guide in Cuzco. A list of licensed guides is available from the Cuzco Tourist Information Office (see "Contact," below).

★GUIDEBOOKS AND MAPS: *The Inca Trail: Cuzco and Machu Picchu*, by Richard Danbury (Trailblazer Guides, www.trailblazer-guides.com, $17.95).

★CONTACT: Cuzco Tourist Information Office (011-51-84-263-176).

JASPER NATIONAL PARK, ALBERTA

Welcome to Canada.
You may never want to leave

With Jasper and Banff National Parks separated only by a road sign that indicates you're leaving one park and entering the other, you might ask, "What's the difference?"

People, for one thing. Jasper has half the number of visitors. And its trail system is perfect for long-distance hikes—if you have the time, fitness level, and backcountry skills needed to cover routes that pass through what one guidebook calls "the premier area for remote wilderness hiking in North America." In other words, climb these trails and you'll be looking down at mountain goats, not tourists.

Several rivers carve valleys through the park, and between them are exquisite mountains that soar past 12,000 feet, casting shadows over the dark fingers of fir and spruce that radiate from acres of subalpine meadows. Trails in the Athabasca River Valley are especially scenic, carrying you into the high country, all the while taking your breath away with stunning vistas of vast glaciers and the turquoise lakes they feed.

The classic Jasper trek is the 27.4-mile Skyline Trail. Make your way from Maligne Lake up the spine of the Maligne Range to a place called The Notch, an 8,136-foot-high cleft in the treeless high country. Even a pilot couldn't hope for a better view of the Rockies. Far below, the Athabasca River sparkles as it runs the wide valley floor under a palisade of sharply cut mountaintops. Move 4 miles down the trail, and you'll startle at the sight of snowcapped Mount Robson. This is what you came for: the highest peak in the Canadian Rockies, twinkling like a crystal canine tooth. Just for you.

FIELD JOURNAL

_____

_____

_____

_____

_____

_____

_____

_____

_____

_____

_____

_____

_____

_____

_____

_____

_____

_____

_____

Expedition Planner

*PERMITS: A day pass costs $6 (Canadian) per person per day or $38 (Canadian) annually. Backcountry campers must also purchase a wilderness pass ($6 [Canadian] per person per night or $42 [Canadian] annually). Campsites can be reserved 3 months in advance for a nonrefundable $10 (Canadian) fee. Call one of the park information centers (see "Contact," opposite page) to reserve your spot.

*ACCESS: Jasper National Park is 192 miles west of Edmonton and 256 miles northwest of Calgary. Buses and trains run to the park from Edmonton. Brewster Transportation (403-762-6767) offers daily service from the Calgary Airport, with drop-offs at some trailheads. From Jasper, take the Yellowhead Highway (also called the Trans-Canada Highway) 3 miles east, then follow Maligne Lake Road for 27.5 miles to the lake. Drive ½ mile past Maligne Lodge to the picnic area and trailhead.

JASPER NATIONAL PARK, AB

_____

_____

_____

_____

_____

_____

_____

_____

_____

_____

_____

_____

_____

_____

_____

_____

_____

_____

_____

_____

_____

*SEASON: Lower-elevation trails open in mid-May; the rest are snow-free by mid-July and usually stay that way until mid-October.

*GEAR: Campfires are not allowed on the Skyline Trail, so bring a backpacker's stove. Bring cold-weather gear, as it can snow here year-round.

*GUIDE SERVICES: Many are available. Call the Jasper Information Centre (see "Contact," at right) for a full list.

*GUIDEBOOKS AND MAPS: For a free backcountry visitor guide, including a trail map, write to the Jasper Information Centre, Trail Office, Jasper National Park, PO Box 10, Jasper, AB T0E 1E0 Canada, or call (780) 852-6176. *Medicine Lake 83C/13* and *Athabasca Falls 83C/12* (Friends of Jasper, 780-852-4767, $12.95 [Canadian]).

*CONTACT: Jasper Information Centre (780-852-6177); Icefield Information Centre (780-852-6288).

KENAI PENINSULA, ALASKA

Float through an
Alaskan wildlife paradise

At more than 3 million acres, Kenai is an embarrassment of riches. The peninsula holds numerous long trails through pine-filled valleys and tundra passes. The southern and eastern sections are as mountainous and glaciated as any corner of the Alaskan frontier. And inside the region's dense forests, where the thick, rain-fed foliage shines in the sunlight, there exists a diversity of creatures to challenge any ecosystem in the hemisphere. If it lives and breathes in Alaska, you'll probably find it somewhere in Kenai.

Or around it. Experts know that you haven't experienced the wilds of Kenai if you haven't paddled a kayak along its salty coastline. The fingerlike coves of Kenai Fjords National Park collect the best of Kenai's beasts in small but potent patches of land. Along the glaciers' edges, you'll glide past puffins and Dall porpoises, while bald eagles hunt fish from above and sea lions tend to their young on nearby rocks. Occasionally, a totem-size bear will materialize from the spruce, approaching the shoreline like an emissary from the high peaks in the distance. After a dozen or so sightings, you may think this area is home to every animal imaginable. Then you remember the one species you haven't seen: humans. Such are the sacrifices of Kenai—hope you can adjust.

FIELD JOURNAL

Expedition Planner

★**PERMITS:** None. Permits are optional, however, in Kenai Fjords National Park.

★**ACCESS:** Follow the Sterling Highway south of Anchorage.

★**GEAR:** No special gear is needed for hiking. For kayaking, rent or bring a kayak, wet suit, and paddle. And don't forget your camera and plenty of film.

★**SEASON:** Go from mid-May through early September, for Alaska's summer highs.

★**GUIDE SERVICES:** Contact Kenai Fjords National Park for a list of licensed outfitters (see "Contact," below).

★**GUIDEBOOKS AND MAPS:** *55 Ways to the Wilderness in Southcentral Alaska*, by Helen D. Nienhueser and John Wolfe, Jr. (The Mountaineers Books, 800-553-4453, $16.95); *The Kenai Canoe Trails*, by Daniel Quick (Northlite Publishing, 907-262-5997, $15.95); *Kenai Fjords National Park and Chugach National Forest #231* and *Kenai National Wildlife Refuge and Chugach National Forest #760* (both from National Geographic Trails Illustrated Maps, 800-962-1643, $9.95 each).

★**CONTACT:** Chugach National Forest (907-743-9500); Chugach State Park (907-345-5014); Kenai Fjords National Park (907-224-3175); Kenai National Wildlife Refuge (907-262-7021).

KILIMANJARO, TANZANIA

Conquer a continent's greatest treasure

Crowned by eternal snows, Kilimanjaro is an overwhelming presence on the African landscape and one of the most dramatic mountains on Earth. The name alone rings with power. To walk up the legendary giant is to undertake the undisputed classic hike of Africa. And to mount its apex is to stand on the roof of a continent.

Though the summit is 19,340 feet above the sea, this is not a technical climb, just a long, uphill slog through semiarid savanna, into a wetlands forest, and onward to the glaciers up top. But what a slog. On the first day, you're surrounded by lush African canopy, draped in greens and muddy browns. When you aren't listening to the shrieks of monkeys in the trees, you might hear the steady rush of a dozen

waterfalls dropping into the valley, or watch multicolored birds swoop from perch to perch while a bearded vulture circles above. Then the trail enters an igneous wasteland littered with boulders, tussock grasses, and hardy miniature flowering plants. Aside from a few oases, this is the scenery that will accompany you to the top.

The most popular trek is the 6-day hike up the Marangu Route, sometimes referred to as the Coca-Cola Route for its relative ease and its pop-

ularity among Westerners. If you prefer to sleep in huts and keep your hands clean, this is the trail for you. But if you're feeling a bit rugged, try the more strenuous, tent-only Machame Route, which winds beneath the glaciers of the mountain's southern face. Here, you'll need all your limbs to vault rocks and boulders as you climb to the beauteous Shira Plateau and then on to the summit, where an entire continent spreads out at your feet.

FIELD JOURNAL

Expedition Planner

★PERMITS: There are numerous park fees that add up to about $70 per person per day, and a mandatory guide service can cost from $700 to a few thousand dollars, depending on the quality of the guide.

★ACCESS: The only direct flight from Europe into Kilimanjaro International Airport is via a KLM flight from Amsterdam. Or fly into Nairobi and take an hour-long connecting flight or a 5-hour shuttle bus ride to Arusha.

★GEAR: You'll need a good pair of boots and, on all routes except Marangu, a zero-degree-Fahrenheit-rated sleeping bag. Prepare for hiking in all weather conditions.

★SEASON: The period from December through March is favored for its warm, clear mornings. June and July are the coldest months.

★GUIDE SERVICES: Hiring a guide is mandatory, and local experts recommend booking one of the more expensive ones. For your money, you'll get a quality guide service that has a permit, treats its staff well, helps you acclimatize to the altitude, and is prepared for emergencies.

★GUIDEBOOKS AND MAPS: *Kilimanjaro & Mount Kenya: A Climbing & Trekking Guide*, by Cameron M. Burns (The Mountaineers Books, 800-553-4453, $18.95).

★CONTACT: Tanzania Tourist Board (212-447-0027).

LOST COAST TRAIL, CALIFORNIA

Find yourself along California's most rugged seashore

Call it a turn for the better. Just north of Fort Bragg, the Pacific Coast Highway leaves the oceanfront and detours 30 miles inland. One look at the jagged cliffs and rugged hills here, and you'll understand why the interstate engineers headed east with their steamrollers, abandoning the water views. Where the coastal road ends, the Lost Coast begins.

The next 50 miles of shoreline rival any stretch in America (North or South). You'll start in Sinkyone Wilderness State Park, where the Lost Coast Trail is more of an undulating jungle hike than a jetty jaunt. The first 17 miles take you on a roller-coaster ride through steep, forested ravines, across bluffs worn smooth by wind, and into isolated coves of fine sand and even finer vistas where saltwater and pine commingle in the expanse. Bring binoculars in the winter and spring, and scan 100 miles of coastline for migrating gray whales. In the final mile of this leg of the trail, the path rises into the Chamisal Mountains, from which you'll see a sweeping panorama of the Pacific's crashing surf.

After a few more miles and a short interlude on asphalt—don't worry, the din of cars will disappear soon enough—you'll come to Black Sands Beach and the northern stretch of the LCT the King Range. Here's the real "coast" of the Lost Coast. For the remaining 25 miles, you'll comb the rough, captivating coastline, watching sea lions bob offshore, sidestepping bear and bobcat tracks on the beach, and feeling in touch with the land and water as never before. Your gratitude, like the horizon sky, will be infinite.

FIELD JOURNAL

_____
_____
_____
_____
_____
_____
_____
_____
_____
_____
_____
_____
_____
_____
_____
_____
_____
_____
_____
_____
_____
_____
_____

Expedition Planner

★PERMITS: When entering Sinkyone, self-register for a permit at the trailhead. The backpacking fee is $2 per person per night; fees for campgrounds vary. Sinkyone designates campsites from Usal to Bear Harbor for overnight stays. In the King Range, you'll need a free fire permit for beach campfires and stove use. Pick one up at the Bureau of Land Management office in Whitethorn, CA, between Shelter Cove and Redway, at 768 Shelter Cove Road.

★ACCESS: The southern Sinkyone trailhead is at Usal Beach, north of Rockport on County Road 431. Trailheads also exist at the top of Sinkyone, Black Sands Beach, and at the very top of the Lost Coast trail near the mouth of Mattole River. Call the Bureau of Land Management or Sinkyone Wilderness State Park (see "Contact," opposite page) for directions.

★SEASON: Head to the coast in the shoulder seasons, spring and fall, which are more like summer than summer. Summer here is windy, foggy, and crowded; winter is wet. With an average of 100 inches of rain annually, this region is the second-wettest spot in the Lower 48.

★GEAR: Hikes in the King Range depend upon the tide table. Several spots are impassable come high tide, or on windy days with high surf. Pick up a tide table at the Bureau of Land Management office, the visitor center at Black Sands Beach, or a local sporting goods store. There are several Shelter Coves in California, so be sure to pick up the chart locally. Bear canisters are required in the King Range. Bring water treatment equipment.

★GUIDE SERVICES: None.

★GUIDEBOOKS AND MAPS: *The Hiker's Hip Pocket Guide to the Mendocino Coast*, by Bob Lorentzen (Bored Feet Press, 707-964-6629, $15); *Lost Coast King Range National Conservation Area* and *Sinkyone Wilderness* maps (both available through the Bureau of Land Management; 707-986-5400; $3 and $1, respectively).

★CONTACT: For the northern section of the trail, in the King Range, contact the Bureau of Land Management (707-986-5400). For the southern section, through the Sinkyone Wilderness, contact Sinkyone Wilderness State Park (707-986-7711).

MOUNT RAINIER
NATIONAL PARK,
WASHINGTON

Trek around the Olympus
of the Northwest

Near sea level on Puget Sound, where millions of bipedal worker ants toil away their daylight hours, many of those lucky enough to have a window cubicle stare wistfully to the southeast. They know that the drizzle will eventually ease, the gray pall will lift, and they'll shout jubilantly, "The mountain is out!" All will stop to stare at the brooding hulk just 60 miles inland, and remember why they love it here.

For hikers, the attraction may be even stronger. It's hard to imagine anyone who walks for pleasure in this corner of the country not feeling the magnetic pull toward Washington's Mount Rainier. Though this active volcano, covered by miles upon miles of glacial ice, is only the fifth-highest mountain in the Lower 48, it rises higher above its base than any other, towering like a 12,000-foot beacon above the city of Longmire. Home to world-record precipitation (Pacific clouds that merely drizzle over Seattle slam full force into Rainier; as they're lifted skyward, rain or snow falls), Mount Rainier National Park also has some of the most scenic trails in the Northwest.

For the complete Rainier experience, there's no beating the 93-mile, round-the-mountain Wonderland Trail. While you may not have time for a full loop, dayhikers shouldn't turn their backpacks on this route. Many of Wonderland's sections offer the best of the whole trail: steep roller-coaster routes that your knees will hate and your eyes will love. While presenting, in sum, nearly 23,000 feet of vertical gain and an equal loss, Wonderland will take you along rich, red huckleberry fields, into creeks and across suspension bridges, up into the alpine air, and back down into the subalpine meadows. Through it all, you'll lose site of Rainier time and again behind bands of gray clouds, but don't let that bother you: Part of the experience is waiting for Her Fickle Majesty to reappear. When she does, you may want to move here.

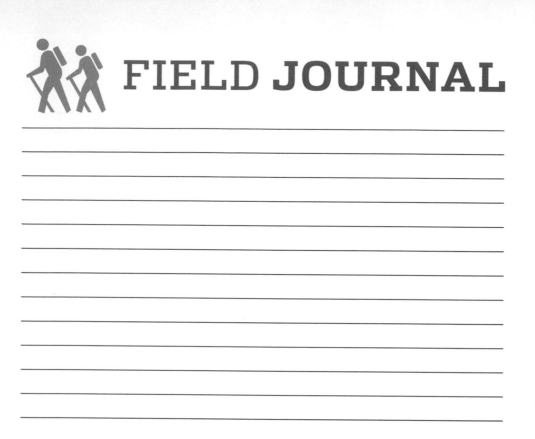

FIELD JOURNAL

_____
_____
_____
_____
_____
_____
_____
_____
_____
_____
_____
_____
_____
_____
_____
_____
_____
_____
_____

MOUNT RAINIER NATIONAL PARK, WA

Expedition Planner

★PERMITS: There's a $10 entrance fee (good for 7 days). The required camping permits are available for free from the park's four visitor centers, including one at Longmire; reservations are not necessary. If you know where you want to camp, however, paying $20 to reserve your campsite in advance is a good idea. If you haven't reserved a spot, be prepared to accept alternate sites.

★ACCESS: Follow I-5 south to exit 120, then follow WA 512 east for 30 miles.

You'll see signs along the way for Mount Rainier National Park. Take WA 7 south 35 miles to WA 706 east. It's 14 miles to the Nisqually entrance. Follow the road to Longmire Station, where you can pick up your camping permit.

★SEASON: Typically, the trail is pretty melted out and the bridges are in place by mid- to late-July. Before then, some stream crossings could prove problematic, and the route should be reserved for adventuresome and experienced wilderness travelers. Be prepared for rain and high-country snow at any moment.

★GEAR: Raingear is a must, as you're practically guaranteed to be rained on for part of your hike. Blue bags are mandatory for collecting human waste. Bring a backpacker's stove.

★GUIDE SERVICES: Though five companies are licensed to lead trips up the mountain, only Cascade Alpine Guides (800-981-0381) offers backpacking trips, including one on the Wonderland Trail. The rest offer rock climbing and mountaineering. In 2004, however, the park plans to increase business on the mountain and offer more guiding permits.

★GUIDEBOOKS AND MAPS: *Hiking Mount Rainier National Park: A Falcon Guide*, by Heidi Schneider and Mary Skjelset (Globe Pequot Press, 800-243-0495, $14.95); *Mount Rainier National Park #217* (National Geographic Trails Illustrated Maps, 800-962-1643, $9.95).

★CONTACT: Mount Rainier National Park (360-569-2211).

MOUNT ST. HELENS NATIONAL VOLCANIC MONUMENT, WASHINGTON

Stand atop a living, breathing volcano

Hike high in the Appalachian Mountains, and you can bet the stones beneath your feet are at least a million years old. Washington's Mount St. Helens is different. Here, the rocks are younger than some college students.

That thought may set your nerves on edge as you ascend the steady incline of Mount St. Helen's Monitor Ridge, gaining about 4,500 vertical feet in less than 5 miles. To the south and east are other volcanoes, pink in the morning's alpenglow; at your feet is the alternately dusty, rocky, and snowy flank of the mountain herself. The ascent is challenging and the views outrageous, but what captures your attention is the mysterious, ragged edge looming above you. This ridge once rose toward a peak. On

May 18, 1980, an earsplitting *bang*, followed by a plume of smoke and ash blasting 60,000 feet, signaled a change to all that.

Today, the 8,363-foot summit takes you to the lip of a crater. Peer over the edge, and you are staring 2,000 feet down at the bulging lava dome of a baby mountain. Ahead is the vast, scabrous plain where, just over 2 decades ago, a forest once stood. Now you find scatterings of adolescent Pa-

cific willow, red alder, and Douglas fir, all packing the field out toward Spirit Lake. And off in the northern distance rise more volcanoes, including the massive 14,411-foot Mount Rainier. The awe and terror mix with surprising ease. This is a true Mount St. Helens moment.

FIELD JOURNAL

_____
_____
_____
_____
_____
_____
_____
_____
_____
_____
_____
_____
_____
_____
_____
_____
_____
_____
_____
_____
_____

Expedition Planner

★PERMITS: Climbing permits are needed to hike above 4,800 feet. From April 1 to October 31, there's a $15-per-person charge to climb; and, from May 15 to October 31, a 100-people-per-day limit. Fifty spots are available for reservation each day (see "Contact," opposite page), and 50 permits for the following day are distributed by lottery at 6 P.M. at Jack's Bar and Grill (360-231-4276) on WA 503, about 23 miles off I-5. A Northwest Forest Pass is required for parking ($5 per day or $30 annually). A backpacking permit is not necessary for overnight trail hiking, except in the Mount Margaret backcountry.

★ACCESS: From exit 21 (Woodland) off I-5, head east on WA 503, which turns into Forest Road 90. Follow 90 for 3 miles, turn left onto Forest Road 83, and turn left again after 5 miles onto Forest Road 81. Go 3 miles, then turn right onto Forest Road 830, a single-lane gravel road that ends at the Ptarmigan trailhead. Park here with your Northwest Forest Pass.

★SEASON: Go from May through October. The snow melts in June, but if you climb before mid-July, you can expect to see snow at some point during your climb.

★GEAR: Ropes aren't required for climbing, but consider taking an ice axe and crampons early in the season. Also, bring gaiters to keep the snow and gravel out of your boots. Some climbers like to bring ski poles regardless of snow cover.

★GUIDE SERVICES: Oregon Peak Adventures (877-965-5100) leads trips up the volcano.

★GUIDEBOOKS AND MAPS: *Mount St. Helens National Volcanic Monument: For Hiking, Climbing, Skiing, and Nature Viewing*, by Klindt Vielbig (The Mountaineers Books, 800-553-4453, $12.95); *Mount St. Helens NW #364S* (Green Trails Maps, 206-546-6277, $3.99).

★CONTACT: Mount St. Helens National Volcanic Monument Headquarters (360-449-7800).

NORTH CASCADES, WASHINGTON

Seek adventure,
and ye shall find Ptarmigan

It's some of the most horizontally challenged ground on the North American continent, gaining (and losing) 11,000 vertical feet along a 35-mile line. No signs direct you through the obscure series of passes. No railings keep you from falling into the crevasses. And no shelters provide refuge from the rains of the Great "Northwet."

But, to paraphrase the saying, with pain comes gain. The Ptarmigan Traverse—a sketchy patchwork of lowland trails and highland cross-country travel in Washington's North Cascades—snakes through mountains that have an ice-smothered grandeur to rival any other range in the Lower 48. Nature knows no subtlety here: You'll stand awestruck by broken glaciers tumbling off Mount Formidable. You'll camp beside the electric glow of nightfall on Kool-Aid Lake. A day later, the emerald sheen of Yang Yang Lakes will welcome you with a Fujichrome vibrancy. By the time you reach Le Conte Glacier, pristine snow will surround you, a reminder that few humans have seen this land from so close.

Along the way, hard-to-find routes will test your backpacking abilities and mountaineering skills, and you may, at times, feel like scuttling home with your tail tucked. But when you've climbed your last airy scramble and crossed your last mound of talus, you'll leave the North Cascades reveling in a triumph of body and soul.

FIELD JOURNAL

Expedition Planner

*PERMITS: Backcountry permits are not required, but vehicles left at trailheads require a Northwest Forest Pass ($5 per day or $30 per year).

*ACCESS: Follow the North Cascades Highway (WA 20) to the town of Marblemount. Turn east on Cascade River Road, and follow it 23 miles to the Cascade Pass trailhead.

*GEAR: Carry crampons, an ice axe, rope, a harness, and prusiks.

*SEASON: Go from mid-July through August. Budget 4 to 5 days for travel, plus a few days for climbing and bad weather.

*GUIDE SERVICES: Try Pro Guiding Service (425-888-6397), a good local outfit with permits and internationally certified guides.

*GUIDEBOOKS AND MAPS: *Cascade Alpine Guide Volume 2: Rainy Pass to Fraser River*, by Fred Beckey (The Mountaineers Books, 800-553-4453, $29.95); U.S. Geological Surveys exist for Cascade Pass, Dome Peak, and Downey Mountain. (USGS, 888-ASK-USGS, $6 each).

*CONTACT: North Cascades National Park, Marblemount Ranger Station (360-873-4590); Darrington Ranger Station (360-436-1155).

OLYMPIC NATIONAL PARK, WASHINGTON

Spend a beach week along the Washington shoreline

There's something about the sound of waves hitting the sand that makes you sleep like a baby. But if you haven't camped on a deserted coastal beach before, you're missing a whole lot more than just some great shut-eye. Things like tide pools filled with 10-legged starfish and shimmering sea anemones, and mornings with laughing seagulls and the sun dancing on the waves. You're missing a climb up a 50-foot cliff to gaze into the ocean's sapphire water and—if you're lucky—to catch a glimpse of a whale breaking the surface a few hundred feet offshore.

These are the kinds of experiences

that await along the Coastal Strip in Washington's Olympic National Park. The 60-mile stretch from Shi-Shi Beach to the Hoh River is the longest tract of virgin coastline left in the Lower 48. You'll hike along a section of white-sand beach, picking your way over ocean-slicked cobblestones and massive, algae-covered logs. When that part ends and a headland juts out into the sea, you'll claw your way up out of the sun and into the cool cedar forests above. Then it's back down to the beach, often via handy rope ladders.

The wonderful up-and-down pattern continues along the entire coast, creating a hike that's varied and beautiful, provided you watch the tides and don't get stranded on the wrong side of a headland. That may sound unlikely, but just wait: With water this captivating, you just never know.

FIELD JOURNAL

OLYMPIC NATIONAL PARK, WA

Expedition Planner

*PERMITS: Available at most ranger stations, permits cost $5 per group plus $2 per adult per night. Call ahead (see "Contact," opposite page) to check quotas and make reservations.

*ACCESS: Use WA 101, which circumnavigates the main body of the park. Access to Shi-Shi Beach is through private property; contact the Makah Information Center (360-645-2201) for details. For a shorter trip, start at Third Beach and hike south for 18 miles to the Hoh River.

*SEASON: Mid-summer brings more stable weather and more hikers. Spring and fall can be wet, but you might have the coast to yourself.

*GEAR: Always come prepared for rain. A good topographical map and tide chart are essential. Campfires are not allowed in some sections; a stove is recommended.

Bear-resistant food canisters are required but can be borrowed from the park with a suggested $3 donation.

⋆**GUIDE SERVICES:** None.

⋆**GUIDEBOOKS AND MAPS:** *100 Hikes in Washington's South Cascades and Olympics: Chinook Pass, White Pass, Goat Rocks, Mount St. Helens, Mount Adams*, by Ira Spring and Harvey Manning (The Mountaineers Books, 800-553-4453, $14.95). Custom Correct's maps of the north and south Olympic Coasts ($3.25 each) are available at park visitor centers, ranger stations, or from the Outdoor Recreation Information Center (206-470-4060).

⋆**CONTACT:** Olympic National Park Wilderness Information Center (360-565-3100).

100-MILE WILDERNESS, MAINE

The Appalachian Trail's most remote forest is your wilderness dream come true

It's as if you're living a meditation. All around you are moonlight, wild conifers, and forest lagoons. The hysterical song of loons echoes somewhere from the dark belly of Lower Jo-Mary Lake. This afternoon, you swam naked in a chilly stream. Tomorrow, a sunrise will wake you, not a blaring alarm clock. And aside from a thru-hiker or two, you will be gloriously alone.

In the entire Northeast, few trails rival 100-Mile Wilderness for sheer remoteness—in fact, almost nothing west of the Rockies compares. Okay, so it's not a technical wilderness; it's part of the Appalachian Trail and is well marked with white blazes. It isn't even 100 miles long (99.4, to be exact). But inexact names and numbers will be the last things on your mind here. You'll be too busy thrilling with every mile you pass, as it dawns on you that you're walking a no-hitter: There's not a single paved or public road between 100-Mile's end points, ME 15 near Monson, Maine, and the Abol Bridge, outside Baxter State Park.

Though you can finish the trail in just over a week, you'll want to take at least 10 days to enjoy all of 100-Mile, from trout-filled Nahmakanta Lake, to the foaming torrents at Little Wilson Falls, to the skyline views from high points like Barren and Chairback Mountains. Start from the south, where the highlands are roughest, and pick up your pace as you hit flatter, more watery terrain. Your finish line will be the Penobscot River, where the reflections of Mount Katahdin and its Baxter brethren will celebrate your victory with silence.

FIELD JOURNAL

Expedition Planner

★PERMITS: There's a fee to access Golden Road, a private toll road between Millinocket and the south entrance to Baxter State Park (on ME 159, a mile north of the North Woods Trading Post); the cost has been $8 per vehicle but could change.

★ACCESS: To reach the southern end, head 3.5 miles out of Monson on ME 15. Access to the northern end is at Abol Bridge via Golden Road.

★SEASON: The prime hiking season runs from early July through early October. Before then, trails can be very muddy; any later and snow may start flying. The Wilderness is busiest in August and early September, when the weather is warmer and drier, the mosquitoes and no-see-ums have dissipated (though not disappeared), and the thru-hikers are on their way north to Katahdin.

★GEAR: To keep the bugs away, bring insect repellent and a tent with no-see-um netting. To protect yourself from *Giardia*, bring a water purification system.

★GUIDE SERVICES: Guides are not permitted on the Appalachian Trail.

★GUIDEBOOKS AND MAPS: *The Appalachian Trail Guide to Maine* (Appalachian Trail Conference, 888-287-8673, $24.95).

★CONTACT: Appalachian Trail Conference (304-535-6331).

OUACHITA NATIONAL FOREST, ARKANSAS/OKLAHOMA

Disappear into the land of lost men

If it's soft country you're after, search elsewhere. These mountains once harbored thieves and horse traders on the lam, and while the bad guys are long buried in a graveyard at nearby Fort Smith, the craggy landscape that hid them proudly defies time's march. But maybe the outlaw in your soul still beckons. If so, a trip through the Ouachita National Forest will feel like a homecoming.

An outdoorsman seeking splendor and solitude will find plenty of both out here. Although it's nestled in a region often dismissed for its monotonous plains, Ouachita is hardly ironing-board flat. The Ouachita Mountains form the spine of the forest's premier hike, the east-west Ouachita Trail,

which undulates between 600 and 2,600 feet in elevation. The trail's 223-mile stretch—192 miles of which are in the national forest proper—takes you over rolling crests and into valleys smothered with oak, hickory, maple, and pine; laced by creeks; and capped with the occasional sandstone rooster comb.

As for solitude, let this be said: Many backpackers have never heard of this stretch, let alone know how to find it. Said guidebook writer Tim Ernst in 2000, "Two years ago, when I hiked the entire trail, I saw a total of four people." In other words, no matter where you lope along the path—from the boulder-strewn, roller-coaster ridges near Tali-hina, Oklahoma, to the piney blue mound of Pinnacle Mountain near Little Rock, Arkansas—expect to lope alone.

FIELD JOURNAL

Expedition Planner

★PERMITS: None.

★ACCESS: The trailhead at the west end of the Ouachita Trail can be accessed at Talimena State Park, about 5 miles north of Talihina, on US 271. The east end of the trail terminates at Pinnacle Mountain State Park, about 12 miles west of Little Rock, on AR 10. Pinnacle Mountain is about 425 miles from Kansas City and 400 miles from St. Louis. Talihina is about 200 miles from Dallas.

★SEASON: The period from October through April is best, although spring or fall is preferable to winter because of the brilliant colors.

★GEAR: No special gear is needed.

★GUIDE SERVICES: None.

★GUIDEBOOKS AND MAPS: *Ouachita Trail Guide*, by Tim Ernst (Cloudland.net, 800-838-4453, $18.95).

★CONTACT: Ouachita National Forest (501-321-5202). You can also contact Talimena State Park (918-567-2052) and Pinnacle Mountain State Park (501-868-5806), where the Ouachita Trail begins and ends, respectively.

OZARK NATIONAL FOREST, ARKANSAS

A slow walk inside a Midwestern dream

Some hikes are about making miles. Others demand a slower pace, softly calling: *Look. Listen. Explore.* In the Ozark Mountains, time seems to hang on the breeze— your ambition slowly disappears as you take in the ancient, eroded tablelands with their mossy boulders, rolling peaks, deep green hickories, and meandering rivers.

It's a good thing, too, because with 1.2 million acres of remote forest to explore, the Ozark National Forest is practically begging to be discovered. In these woods and hollows lie ancient Native American shelters, skyscraping waterfalls, and canyon rim vistas that dare you not to gasp at the grandeur. When the lights go out, it gets even better: The nighttime symphony of hoot owls, whippoorwills, insects, and burping bullfrogs will make you want to applaud (quietly, of course).

Stretching through this middle-American gem is a surprisingly ambitious hike: the 165-mile Ozark Highlands Trail, covering a rocky stretch from neighboring Lake Fort Smith State Park, across the national forest, and out to the banks of the Buffalo National River. Despite the fact that this is one of the premier backpacking routes in the United States, relatively few hikers find their way here each year; far fewer leave their footprints along the entire route. Their loss, your gain. Just remember to save time for weeks of wandering. It's going to be a long, eye-opening trip.

FIELD JOURNAL

Expedition Planner

★PERMITS: None.

★ACCESS: Blazed with white rectangles, the Ozark Highlands Trail is accessible at dozens of trailheads and campgrounds in northwestern Arkansas. The first 6 miles of the trail, which run through Lake Fort Smith State Park, are closed while Fort Smith enlarges the dam and floods the trails. Until those trails are rebuilt, probably in 2006, the westernmost access point is at Dockery's Gap. There is parking at this trailhead on Forest Road 1007, off AR 348.

★SEASON: This is a four-season trail, but summer brings hot, humid days and nights, along with an unpleasant assortment of bugs. Cooler temperatures make spring and fall prime time for hiking; take your pick between lush greenery and autumn colors.

★GEAR: No special gear is needed.

★GUIDE SERVICES: None.

★GUIDEBOOKS AND MAPS: *Ozark Highlands Trail Guide*, by Tim Ernst (Cloudland.net, 800-838-4453, $18.95).

★CONTACT: Ozark National Forest (479-968-2354); Ozark Highlands Trail Association (870-861-5536).

PACIFIC CREST TRAIL

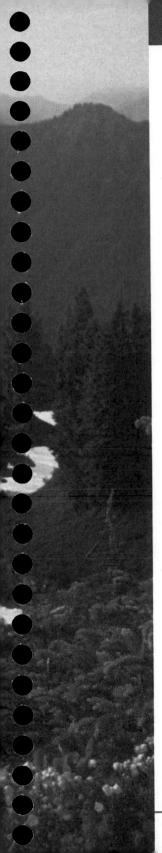

A long walk in sun-drenched forests, alpine wonderlands, and volcano country

Getting high in California is rarely this blissful. Getting low in the rain-soaked Northwest is rarely this thrilling. And walking for months upon months is rarely this energizing.

This is the Pacific Crest Trail, the long, great hike at the end of the North American continent. Travel all 2,650 miles, and you can claim you've seen the best of the West, including the golden Sierra, Oregon's moody blue Crater Lake, and Washington's rugged Cascades.

But let's assume you can't muscle a thru-hike from Mexico to Canada. There are hundreds of trailheads along the PCT, and almost any hike here will reveal superlative scenery. In Oregon, visit the trail's lowest point, near the Bridge of the Gods. You'll skirt the Columbia River before ascending more than 3,000 feet in just 6 miles. When you hit Benson's Plateau, stunning views of Mounts Adams, Rainier, and St. Helens will be waiting.

Or maybe you're closer to the Glacier Peaks Wilderness. If so, walk the path from Suiattle Pass to Stehekin Valley Road. Following the crest of the Cascades, you'll see steep, fractured walls and any of two dozen animals, from eagles to black bears to goats. Quiet groves of soaring old-growth conifers blanket the area below treeline. Above treeline, meadows stretch out beneath tattered ridges and at least a dozen summits cloaked with active glaciers. Cirques and hidden basins hold more than 200 lakes, many unnamed.

And if you can find your way into the rich Sierra, seek out the trail up Forester Pass, where you can rest your boots at 13,180 feet while peering off into Sequoia and Kings Canyon National Parks. Whether you've hiked an afternoon or a month to get here, your everyday life will feel like a distant memory.

FIELD JOURNAL

Expedition Planner

*PERMITS: When hiking more than 500 miles of the PCT at a stretch, pick up a free thru-permit from the Pacific Crest Trail Association (see "Contact," below). Otherwise, you'll need permits from each wilderness area, national park, and forest you cross.

*ACCESS: You can gain access from any road that crosses the trail along the way.

*SEASON: If you're thru-hiking, start at the Mexican border between mid-April and mid-May to ensure you'll reach Canada sometime between mid-September and mid-October, long before winter begins.

*GEAR: If you're thru-hiking, bring an ice axe and enough supplies for 3 to 5 days.

*GUIDE SERVICES: None.

*GUIDEBOOKS AND MAPS: *Guide to the Pacific Crest Trail: Southern California* and *The Pacific Crest Trail: Northern California*, both by Jeffrey Schaffer, Thomas Winnett, Ben Schifrin, and Ruby Johnson Jenkins (Wilderness Press, 800-443-7227, $19.95 each); *The Pacific Crest Trail: Oregon and Washington*, by Jeffrey Schaffer and Andy Selters (Wilderness Press, 800-443-7227, $24.95).

*CONTACT: Pacific Crest Trail Association (916-349-2109).

PARIA CANYON, UTAH/ARIZONA

Explore the desert canyon from heaven

Rays of sunlight decorate the varnished sandstone cliffs along the deep narrows. The liquid trills of canyon wrens add melodic accompaniment to the sounds of water trickling through hanging gardens of fern and monkey flower. No hiker's life is complete without experiencing such desert wonders, and the 38-mile Paria River trek from southern Utah to Lees Ferry in Arizona's Grand Canyon is one of the world's best places to get it all in one gulp.

Most backpackers follow the Paria River for the entire hike, descending from sagebrush flats into the canyon's winding corridors. Slowly, over the course of a few days, the narrow slot of sky overhead widens like a parting curtain. The canyon takes on its Grand cousin's flavor as the trail climbs to benches high above the river for the last 11 miles. Save time for exploring hidden side canyons, prehistoric art panels, abandoned homesteads, lush seep springs, and soaring arches.

Hikers who are more adventuresome should consider beginning their trek at the tributary gorge of Utah's Buckskin Gulch, which stretches the trip to 43 miles. Traversing the incredible 12-mile narrows of the gulch usually involves swimming or wading through several cold pools and lowering packs down a 20-foot cliff. The reward is an otherworldly journey through the longest, narrowest slot canyon in existence.

FIELD JOURNAL

Expedition Planner

★**PERMITS:** Reserve permits up to 6 months in advance; slots go quickly. The cost is $5 per person per day.

★**ACCESS:** From Flagstaff, Arizona, go north on US 89 for about 136 miles, passing through Page. The Paria Contact Station is about 35 miles past Page, in southern Utah. To reach the Buckskin trailhead, continue on US 89 for 4 miles past the information station. Turn south on House Rock Valley Road, and drive 4 more miles. The trailhead is signed and hard to miss.

★**SEASON:** The periods from late March to May, and from late September through November are the best times to travel in this hot country. The flash-flood risk is high from late July through August.

★**GEAR:** You'll be walking through water, so river boots are suggested. Nightly temperatures average between 40° and 50°F, so you may want to pack long underwear and fleece clothing. Fires are not allowed, so bring a backpacker's stove. Hikers are encouraged to bring bags for human-waste disposal.

★**GUIDE SERVICES:** None.

★**GUIDEBOOKS AND MAPS:** The *Paria BLM Hiker's Guide* (Arizona Strip Interpretive Association, 435-688-3246; $8, plus $2 postage); *Hiking and Exploring the Paria River*, by Michael R. Kelsey (Origin Books Sales, $11.95), is available at bookstores.

★**CONTACT:** St. George and Arizona Strip Field Office, Bureau of Land Management (435-688-3200).

ROCKY MOUNTAIN NATIONAL PARK, COLORADO

Take an electric journey through the Colorado wild

To the clap of late afternoon thunder and the splatter of rain, you make up your mind. Fear of stray lightning overwhelms your fear of pushing through a herd of elk—even three bulls brandishing massive racks. Earlier, you watched a bolt sear the ground just across a valley, burning into it like a yellow tornado. Great ionic sky-to-ground exchanges will brand your memories of the park forever.

The next day, you wake to the eerie whistles of bugling elk. All else is silence.

Such are the mysterious extremes of summertime in Rocky Mountain National Park. This park greets more than 3 million visitors each year, but pick the right trail, and you might see no more than half a dozen people in 3 days. You can climb from the west, where the gentle mountainside slopes upward to the Great Divide at a

steady, but manageable, pitch. Or, you can scale the eastern flank, where the mountain is cleaved away into vertical walls 1,000 feet high, as if a giant has taken a monstrous pick-axe to the land.

For a taste of both the easy and the difficult (okay, so nothing is all that easy in the Rockies), head to the remote Mummy Range, which reaches ruggedly into some of the park's most secluded areas. The 9.7-mile Dunraven Trail to Lost Lake, a 2-day trek, starts out easy in neighboring Roosevelt Na-

tional Park. About 7 miles into Rocky Mountain, you'll hit the Lost Falls campsite. Here, the trail picks up intensity, following the north fork of Big Thompson River through Lost Meadow, past snowfields, and up into the preserved, glaciated cliff region. The trail ends at treeline at clear, crisp Lost Lake. Set up camp at the lake—at 10,714 feet, only birds sleep higher in this park.

FIELD JOURNAL

Expedition Planner

*PERMITS: Pick up a $15 backcountry pass, good for 7 nights, at the backcountry office at the Beaver Meadow Visitor Center. The entrance fee is $5 per person for 7 days for those entering on a bicycle or motorcycle, $15 for those entering in a car. An annual pass is $30. You can also use your National Parks Pass or Golden Pass (Age, Eagle, and Access).

*ACCESS: Rocky Mountain National Park is 70 miles northwest of Denver. Follow CO 36 through Lyons. In Estes Park, turn right onto MacGregor Avenue/Devil's Gulch Road. Go past the Glenhaven Post Office, then turn left onto Dunraven Glade Road. The Dunraven trailhead is at the end of the road.

*SEASON: Go from July through early October, when the trails are free of snow. Lightning storms occur almost daily in the summertime. Be off the summits by noon. In the winter, there is the potential for avalanches. Be sure to ask rangers about current conditions, and stay away from steep slopes.

*GEAR: Wear sunglasses with ultraviolet and infrared protection; regular shades aren't enough at this elevation. Carry water treatment supplies to rid your drinking water of *Giardia*. If you're hiking from December to March, you'll need gear that will protect you from temperatures of -35°F or below. Carrying a transceiver, a portable shovel, ski poles, and an avalanche cord will increase your chances of surviving an avalanche.

*GUIDE SERVICES: None.

*GUIDEBOOKS AND MAPS: *Hiking Rocky Mountain National Park: A Falcon Guide*, by Kent and Donna Dannen (Globe Pequot Press, 800-243-0495, $14.95); *Rocky Mountain National Park #200* (National Geographic Trails Illustrated Maps, 800-962-1643, $9.95).

*CONTACT: Rocky Mountain National Park (970-586-1206). For the backcountry office, call (970) 586-1242.

SEQUOIA AND KINGS CANYON NATIONAL PARKS, CALIFORNIA

Visit the quiet giants of America's premier forest

Consider John Muir's introduction to the stately sequoias: "When I entered this sublime wilderness, the day was nearly done; the trees with rosy, glowing countenances seemed to be hushed and thoughtful . . . and one naturally walked softly and awestricken among them." To recreate Muir's emotional experience, head for Sequoia and Kings Canyon National Parks in the southern Sierra. Deep in the parks' backcountry, at Redwood Meadow, you can still experience the big trees as Muir did—in the wilderness, full of wonder, and without carloads of camera-wielding tourists.

In a way, Sequoia and Kings are almost too perfect. Even if the world's biggest trees didn't live here, you'd still have the highest mountain in the Lower 48 (Whitney) and, arguably, the deepest canyon in the United States (Kings). But because most backpackers zero in on the latter two, you should head straight for the sequoias, where you'll walk slack-jawed among 2,000-year-old giants with names like General Sherman and General Grant.

The most direct route to Redwood Meadow is a 15.7-mile, one-way trail along the Middle Fork of the Kaweah River. You'll start low and ascend gradually past oaks and chaparral, sneaking up into the shade, and skirting the Kaweah River Gorge amid endless views of the 12,000-foot crest of the Great Western Divide. Before you realize it, you'll pop through an invisible door at 6,000 feet into a towering grove of sequoia. Lie at the base of these forest behemoths, stare up at the massive stalks of cinnamon-red bark, and be "awestricken."

FIELD **JOURNAL**

_____

_____

_____

_____

_____

_____

_____

_____

_____

_____

_____

_____

_____

_____

_____

_____

_____

_____

_____

Expedition Planner

★PERMITS: Permits are required for backcountry camping and cost $15 per hiking party. From May 21 to September 21, the park has a quota system, which limits the number of hikers on each trail. Roughly two-thirds of those slots may be reserved ahead, while the rest are handed out on a first come, first served basis each day. There is also an entrance fee of $10 per vehicle.

★ACCESS: Take CA 198 east into Sequoia and Kings Canyon National Parks. At the entrance in Three Rivers, CA 198 turns into a park road called Generals Highway. One mile past the entrance, stop at the wilderness office and pick up your permit. Continue driving for about 7 miles. At Hospital Rock, turn right toward the Buckeye Campground. At the fork in the road, bear left toward the Middle Fork Trailhead.

★SEASON: For lower-elevation hikes like the one to Redwood Meadow, springtime is beautiful when the wildflowers start to bloom and the vegetation hasn't yet turned golden and dry. Do the Middle Fork Trail in spring or early fall; come July and August, the full sun will be beating on the trail—

with little shade, it will be too hot to hike. Wait for the snowmelt to clear at higher elevations, typically at the end of June.

*GEAR: Bear-resistant canisters are required in some parts of the park; rent one at the Foothills Visitor Center. You can also store your food using the counterbalance method, though many bears have figured out how to foil this system—use a bear canister to be safe.

*GUIDE SERVICES: None.

*GUIDEBOOKS AND MAPS: *Hiking Sequoia and Kings Canyon National Parks*, by Laurel Scheidt (Globe Pequot Press, 800-243-0495, $16.95); *Sequoia and Kings Canyon National Parks Recreation Map*, by Tom Harrison (Tom Harrison Maps, 800-265-9090, $8.95); *Sequoia/Kings Canyon National Parks #205* (National Geographic Trails Illustrated Maps, 800-962-1643, $9.95).

*CONTACT: Sequoia and Kings Canyon National Parks (559-565-3341). For the backcountry office, call (559) 565-3766.

SIERRA NEVADA,
CALIFORNIA

There's golden views in these here mountains

Want to find a drop-dead gorgeous hike in California's Sierra Nevada? Pin a map of the Sierra to the wall, blindfold yourself, and throw a dart at the map. If you hit paper, you've found your hike. This is one of the finest backpacking landscapes on the planet, and every trailhead is a bull's-eye.

Want proof we're not exaggerating? Spend a week here. Meander past painted meadows and brilliant-white granite outcroppings. Stand in the shadow of massive, craggy peaks. Bask in the Sierra sunshine. Then do it again. And again. And again. Sublime beauty isn't found in rare or isolated moments in the Sierra. It surrounds you for as many miles or days as you can spare.

A lot of wilderness-loving Californians flock to a handful of Sierra hot spots every summer weekend. Don't let the crowds deter you. Some 400 miles long, the Sierra hides its nooks and crannies well: If you aim for these, you'll meet few, if any, backcountry wanderers.

The Corral Valley Trail in the Carson-Iceberg Wilderness is such a place. You'll hike through open sagebrush past watery creeks, meadows full of wildflowers, coniferous forests, western pine, and one of the largest western juniper trees in the Sierra. The streams here jump with Piaute cutthroat trout. Irises grow wild, and the paintbrushes mix together to form a radiant panorama. Shooting stars will line the path by day and fly overhead by night. And the sounds you hear in the darkness won't come from neighboring tents, but from coyotes yipping at each other across the valley.

FIELD JOURNAL

Expedition Planner

*PERMITS: The free, self-administered Wilderness Visitor's Permit is found at the trailheads.

*ACCESS: From US 395, take Mill Canyon Road, 1.3 miles north of Walker, CA. Turn right onto Golden Gate Road, and follow the signs for the Little Antelope Pack Station. Go 6.3 miles to a signed junction, and turn left for the Corral Valley trailhead.

*SEASON: The best wildflower display is in June. The best hiking is after the snowpack melts, usually by the end of June.

*GEAR: Remember the Sierra's typical afternoon thunderstorms, and remember your raingear. Consider bringing a bear-resistant canister.

*GUIDE SERVICES: None for backpacking.

*GUIDEBOOKS AND MAPS: *Carson-Iceberg Wilderness,* by Jeffrey Schaffer (Wilderness Press, 800-443-7227, $14.95). *Carson-Iceberg Wilderness Map* (U.S. Department of Agriculture, Forest Service; $6.42); call the district ranger (see "Contact," below) for a copy.

*CONTACT: Carson Ranger District (775-882-2766).

WATERTON LAKES
NATIONAL PARK, ALBERTA

Get up and away for super views of Canada and beyond

A message from hikers who know Waterton Lakes National Park and its Carthew Ridge: *Pity those who turn back too soon.* The first few miles of the Carthew hike are pretty but plain, switchbacking through old-growth subalpine fir. Bear with it, though, and the payoff appears: a smorgasbord of Waterton's varied habitats, sampled from 7,950 feet.

Your first hint comes when the forest thins by Summit Lake, a beautiful alpine tarn offering stunning views of Mount Custer's and Chapman Peak's massive headwalls. Swinging north, the route ascends through waves of white-flowered bear grass swaying in the breeze, then through mauve scree to windblown Carthew Ridge.

One glance and you'll understand why the ridge is known locally as Carthew Summit: Although the mountain's true summit is still a scramble away, the vistas here are, in a word, spectacular. Glacier National Park's tallest peak, 10,466-foot Mount Cleveland, dominates the eastern horizon. To the southwest loom two more of Glacier's remote high peaks, Kintla and Kinnerly. Under Chapman's north wall, Hudson Glacier's meltwater turns Lake Nooney a striking blue.

It's the northeast view, though, that confirms Waterton's powerful sense of place. Here, just 10 miles out, you see mountains that, devoid of foothills, spout upward from the prairie with the subtlety of a moon shot. Spot a grizzly bear emerging from a valley to reclaim its ancestral home on the high plains, and your skywalk will be complete.

FIELD JOURNAL

Expedition Planner

*PERMITS: Permits cost $8 (Canadian) per person per night. Camping is in designated sites only, with four tent sites at Alderson Lake. Reservations are available up to 90 days in advance for a $12 (Canadian) fee. The park also charges an entry fee of $5 per adult or $12.50 per group.

*ACCESS: Drive to the town of Waterton Park, 32 miles west of Cardston, at the western terminus of AB 5, and 4 miles north of the international border. From here, you'll have to hop a shuttle to take you to the beginning of the Carthew-Alderson hike.

*SEASON: Early July through September. Snowy slopes can be a hazard year-round, as it can snow any day of the year.

*GEAR: Sturdy hiking boots and trekking poles come in handy for rough spots on the trail and for negotiating the long descent. Wind is often a factor on the crest. Pack a shell and insulating layers suitable for high-mountain weather. Fires are not allowed, so bring a stove. Bear spray is recommended.

*GUIDE SERVICES: White Mountain Adventures (800-408-0005).

*GUIDEBOOKS AND MAPS: *Hiking Glacier and Waterton Lakes National Parks: A Falcon Guide*, by Erik Molvar (Globe Pequot Press, 800-243-0495, $14.95); *Waterton Lakes National Park* (Parks Canada, 403-859-5133, call for price).

*CONTACT: Waterton Lakes National Park (403-859-5133).

WHITE MOUNTAIN NATIONAL FOREST, NEW HAMPSHIRE

All hail the Presidentials

Spectacular, challenging, overwhelming: Adjectives fail to capture the magnificence of the White Mountains' King Ravine Trail. A great crescent of alpine exposure, this premier climb just off the Appalachian Trail will test your constitution with the longest above-tree-line ridge, and the worst weather east of the Rockies. Winds will test your balance, and clouds may limit your visibility to 100 yards as you ascend. The payoff is a review of American history, delivered one 5,000-foot peak at a time: Jefferson, Adams, Madison. And, of course, Washington, the highest climb in the Northeast; on a clear day, you'll see five states from here.

To visit the Presidentials, depart from Lowes Path and forge upward through hardwood forests, shattered boulders, and gushing waters. A bit farther, the trail forks, forcing you to choose: Will you take The Subway, a belly-crawling obstacle course, or the Elevated Trail, a mere scamper by comparison? Either way, the path leads to the Ice Caves Loop, which winds through deep, glacial caves where snow and ice linger year-round.

Then comes the headwall. You'll scuttle up rock and rubble, gaining 1,000 vertical feet in ½ mile, before hitting the trail's plateau. Catch your breath and admire the Presidentials. Even with the wind in your face, the view will have you standing at attention.

Note: Among the Presidentials is a mountain named Clinton. Lest you think it's the namesake of our 42nd president, you should know it was named in the 1800s.

FIELD JOURNAL

*GUIDE SERVICES: North Conway, New Hamsphire, roughly 20 miles south of the Presidentials, has one of the highest concentrations of guides in the country. Try Bartlett Adventures (603-374-0866) or New England Mountain Guides (207-935-2008).

*GUIDEBOOKS AND MAPS: *White Mountain Guide: Hiking Trails in the White Mountain National Forest*, edited and compiled by Gene Daniell and Jon Burroughs (Appalachian Mountain Club, 800-262-4455, $21.95).

*CONTACT: The Appalachian Mountain Club's Pinkham Notch Visitor Center (603-466-2721); Androscoggin Ranger District (603-466-2713).

WRANGELL–ST. ELIAS
NATIONAL PARK AND
PRESERVE, ALASKA

Disappear into the largest wilderness in the United States

Your heart is pounding and your stomach churning as your charter plane banks and drops toward Grizzly Lake, but it isn't the bumpy Cessna that has you queasy: It's the sheer vastness of the wild place you are about to enter. Alaska's Wrangell–St. Elias is the largest national park in the United States; and, therefore, an undeniable rite of passage. If you've explored Wrangell, call yourself a backpacker—you've earned it.

The best place to begin is Jacksina Creek Valley, just one of the countless pockets of perfect wilderness here. When the plane has droned off, take a deep breath and look around in silence. This remote valley has it all: snowcapped peaks looming in the distance, 360 degrees of Dall sheep–dotted slopes and plateaus, a broad tundra floor laced with moose and bear tracks, the roiling Jacksina Creek flanked by wide swaths of gravel, and a glorious glacier.

As this is Alaska, don't expect a bevy of trails. Instead, put your route-finding skills to the test and wander. Travel the interior, where the wildlife is thick and varied, and you might cross paths with a herd of caribou or a grizzly bear scrounging for blueberries. You'll see marmots peeking out from their rocky dens. Overhead, golden and bald eagles will soar. At night, when the temperature drops, you'll be tempted to climb into the warm sanctuary of your tent. But does a backpacker choose sleep over watching the northern lights? Take an hour to stargaze as the sky dances in waves of color. Your dreams won't compare.

FIELD JOURNAL

WRANGELL–ST. ELIAS NATIONAL PARK AND PRESERVE, AK

Expedition Planner

★PERMITS: None, though rangers recommend that you submit a backcountry itinerary at the visitor center or any of the ranger stations.

★ACCESS: The park keeps a list of licensed bush pilots. Fly into Anchorage, then charter an air taxi to Glennallen. You can get to the northern part of the park by renting a car and going northeast on AK 1. *Note:* Some car rental places forbid clients to take their cars here.

★SEASON: The hiking season extends from late June to late August, though an early snowmelt or late snowfall may extend the season in either direction. Avoid bugs by going in late August or early September. Be prepared for any kind of weather. Hunting season is from August 10 to September 20, and Grizzly Lake is a prime hunting destination, so wear bright colors.

★GEAR: Bring a backpacker's stove, as wood is scarce, and a bear-resistant canister. If you're heading to the coast, grab a tide table. If you're hitting any of the park's 2,000 glaciers, carry an ice axe, crampons, and rope.

★GUIDE SERVICES: Contact the park (see "Contact," at right) for a list of licensed guides.

★GUIDEBOOKS AND MAPS: *Hiking in Wrangell–St. Elias*, by Danny Kost (Alaska Natural History Association, 907-274-8440, $13.95); *Wrangell–St. Elias National Park and Preserve #249*, (National Geographic Trails Illustrated Maps, 800-962-1643, $9.95); *United States Geological Survey: Nabesna A-5*, (USGS, 888-ASK-USGS, $6).

★CONTACT: Wrangell–St. Elias National Park and Preserve (907-822-5234).

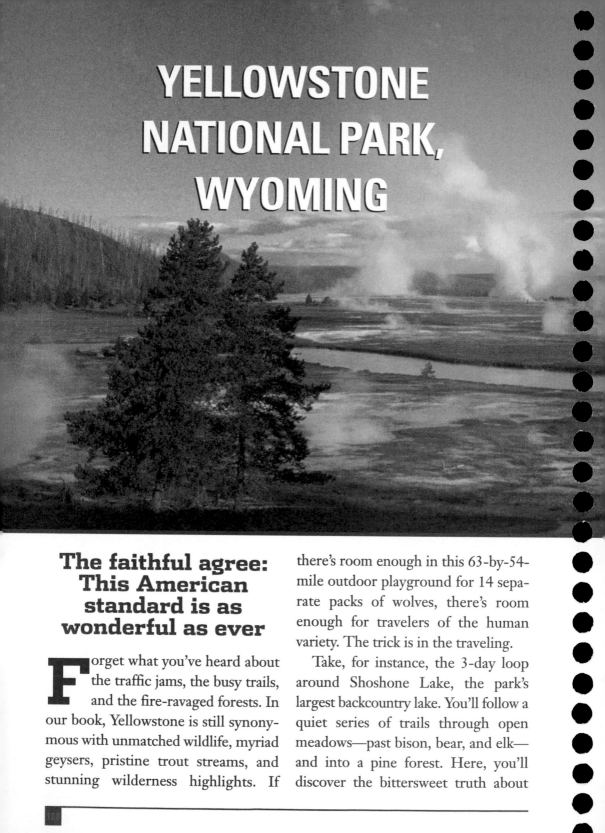

YELLOWSTONE NATIONAL PARK, WYOMING

The faithful agree: This American standard is as wonderful as ever

Forget what you've heard about the traffic jams, the busy trails, and the fire-ravaged forests. In our book, Yellowstone is still synonymous with unmatched wildlife, myriad geysers, pristine trout streams, and stunning wilderness highlights. If there's room enough in this 63-by-54-mile outdoor playground for 14 separate packs of wolves, there's room enough for travelers of the human variety. The trick is in the traveling.

Take, for instance, the 3-day loop around Shoshone Lake, the park's largest backcountry lake. You'll follow a quiet series of trails through open meadows—past bison, bear, and elk—and into a pine forest. Here, you'll discover the bittersweet truth about

Yellowstone fires: For all the destruction and death they cause, the scenery they leave can be startlingly beautiful. To be exact, four major fires have hit this area in the past 125 years, leaving a mosaic of charred lodgepole pines, pink fireweed, and fresh trees, some already a dozen feet into their adolescence.

Keep going and you'll eventually hit Shoshone Lake's western end, where the pristine Shoshone Geyser Basin is crowded not by day-trippers but by 110 thermal features in a mile-long parade of burbling mud and roiling springs. After a short wait at Minute Man Geyser—this cousin of Old Faithful spouts every 1 to 3 minutes—wend your way around the basin's hot spots and into Shoshone Meadow, where dime-size strawberries and Silvery lupines await. Then stand among them and revel: At this moment, all of Yellowstone is yours alone.

FIELD JOURNAL

_____
_____
_____
_____
_____
_____
_____
_____
_____
_____
_____
_____
_____
_____
_____
_____
_____
_____
_____
_____
_____
_____
_____
_____
_____

Expedition Planner

★PERMITS: A free backcountry permit is required for all overnight trips; you can pick one up in person 48 hours before your hike or reserve one a year in advance for a fee of $20. All applications must come by mail; call 307-344-2160 to request the proper forms. A park pass, which is also valid at Grand Teton National Park, is $20 per vehicle for 7 days. Or use your National Parks Pass or Golden Pass (Age, Eagle, and Access) for entry.

★ACCESS: Fly into Cody or Jackson, Wyoming; Bozeman or Billings, Montana; or Idaho Falls, Idaho. Bus service is available from Bozeman to West Yellowstone, Montana, and commercial transportation to the park is available from Cody and Jackson. While many entrances are open seasonally, the north entrance of the park is open year-round. The DeLacy Creek

Trailhead is on the park road between Old Faithful and Grant Village.

*SEASON: Head to Yellowstone after the snow melts out, which should happen by July, and before the snow and cold weather set in in mid-September.

*GEAR: Bring bear spray.

*GUIDE SERVICES: Contact rangers (see "Contact," at right) for a list of local guides.

*GUIDEBOOKS AND MAPS: *Yellowstone Trails*, by Mark Marschall (Yellowstone Association, 877-967-0090, $11.95); *Yellowstone National Park #201* (National Geographic Trails Illustrated Maps, 800-962-1643, $9.95).

*CONTACT: Yellowstone National Park (307-344-7381).

YOSEMITE NATIONAL
PARK, CALIFORNIA

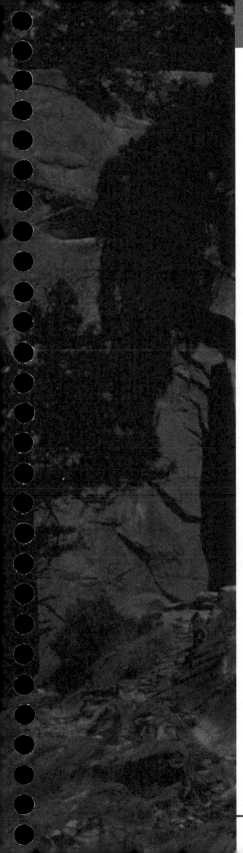

The treasure of the Sierra still shines

Here she is: John Muir's spiritual home, the center of the 1970s backpacking boom, poster child for overcrowded parks, and the source of that addictive Ansel Adams light. For a century, California's Yosemite National Park has both delighted and frustrated. Love it or hate it, though, few can ignore its seductive whisper: *Come. Visit.*

Trust that voice: Yosemite won't disappoint. Even before your boots hit dirt in Yosemite, your senses will cry uncle from the onslaught of scenery. Monstrous white cliffs in Yosemite Valley, sky-piercing summits in the backcountry, vanilla-scented pine forests at every trailhead, creeks that slide in sheets across polished granite slabs before shooting into space—the wonders never cease.

When you're here, myriad hiking options lay before you: scores of trails covering 800 miles; six life zones ranging from chaparral to alpine tundra. Where do you start?

Avoid famous options like the busy High Sierra Camp circuit. Instead, take a 4-day walk in the southern part of Cathedral Range. You'll pass hours watching shadows curl around the tips of the rocky crests above as if they were great sundials jutting into the sky. Along the Merced River, you'll stare in wonder at how such an immense body of swift-moving water can be so silent. And when you see a bear rear on its hind legs in the distance, remind yourself that he's the first two-legged creature you've seen on this trip. Somewhere, John Muir is nodding his approval.

FIELD JOURNAL

_____
_____
_____
_____
_____
_____
_____
_____
_____
_____
_____
_____
_____
_____
_____
_____
_____
_____
_____

Expedition Planner

*PERMITS: Free wilderness permits are required for all overnight stays in Yosemite's backcountry. Half the permits can be reserved through the Wilderness Office (209-372-0740); the other half are issued up to 24 hours in advance. The entrance fee to the park is $20 per car for 7 days, $40 for an annual pass. Spaces for the John Muir Trail are given out by lottery. You may also use your National Parks Pass or Golden Pass (Age, Eagle, and Access) for entry.

*ACCESS: From Los Angeles or Fresno, follow CA 41 into the park's southern en-

trance. From San Francisco, follow CA 120 into one of the park's western entrances. From San Jose, follow CA 140 into the other western entrance.

*SEASON: The period from June through September is prime hiking season. In June and July, you'll find bigger waterfalls, more flowers, and more bugs. To get into the high country, wait until the snow melts out, which should happen around July. Such spectacular waterfalls as Yosemite Falls, the world's fifth tallest, dry up by August. September tends to be even drier.

*GEAR: Bring a bear-resistant food canister; you can rent or buy one at the visitor center. Canisters are recommended in some areas but required in others, such as alpine regions, where there are no trees to counterbalance your food. Whether there are trees around or not, you should use a canister. The black bears here can crack the counterbalance method: it's a delay tactic, not a bear-proof solution to food storage. Remember iodine tablets or some sort of filter to treat your water.

★**GUIDE SERVICES:** Southern Yosemite Mountain Guides (800-231-4575); Yosemite Mountaineering School (209-372-8344); Yosemite Guides (877-425-3366). Though Yosemite Guides is much smaller than the other two outfits, its guides are trained more in geology and natural features than in the basics of hiking.

★**GUIDEBOOKS AND MAPS:** *Yosemite National Park*, by Jeffrey Schaffer, includes topographic maps (Wilderness Press, 800-443-7227, $18.95); *Yosemite National Park #206* (National Geographic Trails Illustrated Maps, 800-962-1643, $9.95).

★**CONTACT:** Yosemite National Park (209-372-0200).

ZION NATIONAL PARK, UTAH

Some call it heaven. You'll call it Utah's finest

Zion Canyon has been called a Yosemite Valley in red. It's a compliment, sure, but even a Yosemite comparison doesn't do justice to this deep, sheer-walled crevasse. In southern Utah's magical canyon country, where vast and varied scenery is the only constant, Zion stands as the boldest and most beautiful.

If you doubt our good word, venture to Zion National Park, where the cliffs rise thousands of vertical feet in white, yellow, and red walls of sandstone so brilliant that the first visitors to this place believed it to be God's divine work. (The names of Zion's gigantic rock formations reflect those visitors' religiously inspired awe: West Temple, Towers of the Virgin, Angels Landing, The Great White Throne, etc.) With all due respect to God, the master architect in Zion is the Virgin River, which has spent the past 13 million years carving this land. Today, the unassuming river wends its way along the canyon floor amid Fremont cottonwoods, willows, and velvet ashes.

Zion Canyon is awash in human activity, so its trails are busy—but worthwhile nonetheless. Challenge your heart rate and take the steep path to Angels Landing, where the airy summit's sweeping views will thrill you long after you regain your breath. Or beat the crowds by trekking to Kolob Canyons, in the park's northwest corner, where cool forests of pinyon and juniper trees cap the deep rifts and sandstone cliffs. Either way, the experience is heavenly.

FIELD JOURNAL

Expedition Planner

★PERMITS: Permits are required for overnights and some daytrips in the backcountry. Prices vary, but expect to pay between $10 and $20 for your party. Access to the park is $20 per vehicle for 7 days, while an annual pass is $40. You can pick up a permit up to 3 days before your hike.

★ACCESS: Zion Canyon is along UT 9 in southwestern Utah, 46 miles from the airport at St. George; the south entrance is through Springdale, and the east entrance is west of Mount Carmel Junction. The Kolob Canyons Visitor Center can be reached from exit 40 off I-15.

★SEASON: The ideal hiking seasons are spring and fall, when temperatures are moderate—often 80°F during the day and in the 40s at night. From June through August, it's generally too hot for hiking, with the mercury soaring above 90°F or even 100°F. Winters are relatively mild, and the ground in Zion Canyon is typically snow-free, although snow does accumulate on the plateaus, where trails can be snowpacked and icy.

*GEAR: Campfires are not allowed, so bring a backpacker's stove. Also bring a water purifier.

*GUIDE SERVICES: None. Commercial guide services are not permitted on any trail or route within the park.

*GUIDEBOOKS AND MAPS: *Hiking Zion and Bryce Canyon National Parks: A Falcon Guide*, by Erik Molvar and Tamara Martin (Globe Pequot Press, 800-243-0495, $14.95); *Zion National Park # 214* (National Geographic Trails Illustrated Maps, 800-962-1643, $9.95).

*CONTACT: Zion National Park (435-772-3256).

Photo Credits